my nepenthe

My NEPENTHE

Bohemian Tales of Food, Family, and Big Sur

Romney Steele

Photography by Sara Remington

Andrews McMeel
Publishing, LLC
Kansas City • Sydney • London

Big Sur has this intoxicating allure, draws you in, holds you, and never wants to let you go. When you're in Big Sur, you're forced to enjoy the simple things in life, the things most important to me and most important to this book: food, family, art, and nature.

— SARA REMINGTON

10 11 12 13 14 SDB 11 10 9 8 7 6 5 4 3 2

Library of Congress Cataloging-in-Publication Data

Steele, Romney.
  My Nepenthe : Bohemian Tales of Food, Family, and Big Sur / Romney Steele ; photography by Sara Remington.
    p. cm.
  Includes bibliographical references and index.
  ISBN-13: 978-0-7407-7914-5
  ISBN-10: 0-7407-7914-1
  1. Nepenthe Restaurant—History. 2. Cookery, American—California style. 3. Steele, Romney. I. Title.

TX945.5.N38S74 2009
641.59794—dc22

2009013259

www.andrewsmcmeel.com
www.mynepenthebook.com

Design by Lisa Berman
Styling Assistant: Tina Snow

Photo Credits: pages 30–31, 35: Morley Baer © 2009 by the Morley Baer Photography Trust, Santa Fe (page 30–31: Lee Harbick Collection, California History Room, Monterey Public Library); page 121: Walter Chappell; page 117: Tenny Chonin; pages 2, 47, 100, 322–23: Brooke Elgie; pages 56–57, 88–89, 100 (top): J.R. Eyerman, Time & Life Pictures, Getty Images; page 29: Lewis Josselyn; page 44: Ben Lyons; page 41: Heidi McGurrin; all other historical images and illustrations are courtesy of the Fassett family, or by author.

ATTENTION: SCHOOLS AND BUSINESSES
Andrews McMeel books are available at quantity discounts with bulk purchase for educational, business, or sales promotional use. For information, please write to: Special Sales Department, Andrews McMeel Publishing, LLC, 1130 Walnut Street, Kansas City, Missouri 64106.

In memory of my grandparents,
Bill and Lolly Fassett

To Trevor and Nicoya, with love,
and for my family

Contents

{ *Introduction* }

What Dreams Are Made Of

Perched on the Big Sur cliffs 808 feet above the Pacific Ocean in California, Nepenthe Restaurant boasts sweeping views of the rugged Santa Lucia mountain range and the wild south coast of Monterey County. Angular mountains plunge into the crashing surf below, and on a clear day there is no limit to the scenery, unspoiled and immense in nature. Opened in 1949 by my maternal grandparents, the restaurant is nestled among native oak trees and a historic log cabin (now faced by brick) once owned by Orson Welles and Rita Hayworth, which has been our family home since 1947. The original property was 12 acres and the family holdings have since grown to 37 acres of land, with multiple structures added over the years.

Sixty years on, Nepenthe's design, with its integrated architecture, vivid patio, and terraced landscaping, remains as modern and unique as it was when it was built. Rock gardens brim with native and drought-tolerant plants, and wild sage and lavender permeate the walkways. The treasure-filled Phoenix Shop below the restaurant and its rooftop café are now deeply imbedded in place, and just as much a part of the Nepenthe experience.

✦

Growing up at Nepenthe, I recall no singular moment of awe at seeing the view for the first time, no marveling at the experience in the same way as someone visiting. For those of us who grew up on the property, Nepenthe was not a novelty; it was our home. Little changed when we woke each morning, except for the weather. The restaurant opened its doors daily, the sharp hills against a backdrop of sea and sky remained ever-present. Our moment of awe, instead, was when guests arrived: the famous and not so famous, the movie stars, writers, travelers, old friends, and "rugged individualists," as my grandmother called the many colorful people who passed through Nepenthe's doors. "How many people will show up today?" we wondered, or "Look who just walked across the terrace," we'd shout, then line up on my grandmother's row of chenille-covered beds to watch through the windows.

Our Nepenthe was largely a theatre show, the terrace a grand stage and the guests unwitting players in our production. I loved the costumes, the nightly dancing, and the dressing up and occasionally pretending to be a customer, the waiters going along with my game. I occasionally pine for the childhood experience, to dance once more in circles under the lights, my arms outstretched, without a care in the world.

When I was in my early thirties, and living in Henry Miller's cabin on Big Sur's Partington Ridge with two young children and working as a pastry chef at Sierra Mar Restaurant, I started thinking about writing my family's story. There at the same massive table where Henry shared meals with family and friends, the idea took hold.

Yet, honestly, I didn't know the shape or form it would take, and didn't anticipate the agony and wonder of unearthing family tales (not least my own), nor all the work it would take to compile all the recipes, down to the last teaspoon of salt in a pot of soup. I spent countless hours in my cousin Erin's archive room in the family cabin, going through old papers and letters she had neatly organized in files. I dug through dozens of boxes in the back shed at Nepenthe, sorted through hundreds of old photographs, read my grandmother's letters and correspondence to and from my grandfather, and tracked down my family's history in libraries and search engines from Carmel to San Francisco to New York.

This is not the definitive Nepenthe story or even an unbiased account, but the way I experienced it, or in some cases, chose to retell it. It is *my* Nepenthe. Everyone has their *own* Nepenthe experience, their own unique stories to tell. I hope that each of you find some of *your* Nepenthe within the pages of this book. Surely there will be moments of dissent, when someone reads something and says it isn't so. I have tried to write only what I know is true, or otherwise allude as much.

It has been many years since I lived and worked at Nepenthe, but it is never far from my heart. All along this story has been simmering, like a big pot of soup on the back burner. Inspired by my passion for food and cooking, combined with the physical urge to write it all down, put words on paper, paint on canvas, this book, in fact, has been in the making for many years.

My Nepenthe is as much about my family's restaurant as it is about my family, and it recounts our more than sixty years on the coast. It is about my grandparents, Bill and Lolly Fassett, their five children, and their grandchildren. My grandparents' own stories: how they met, where they come from, and insights as to how and what their dreams were made of, are included along with a brief section about my grandmother's stay as a young woman on the island of Capri, Italy, where she lived out an earlier dream before claiming her *own* Nepenthe.

The stories include Nepenthe's colorful history as a gathering place, a noted bohemian haunt; its foray into the film industry during the shooting of *The Sandpiper,* featuring Elizabeth Taylor and Richard Burton; the colorful scene that played out in the 1960s and into the '70s; and onward through to this decade, as the family still owns and operates the family enterprise, and where I highlight Nepenthe's unique relationship with Pisoni Vineyards.

I could have written a whole other book just on the bohemian scene at Nepenthe, and another one on the artists and writers who made up that particular time in Big Sur, imbuing it with so much life and fervor. It is what most people ask about and revere when they write about us, and it is true that it was a compelling part of our history and the most fun to write about. Artists and writers, especially Henry Miller, are woven into the pages of *My Nepenthe*, as well as countless other characters. This early time and the culture of place undisputedly changed the landscape and minds of fellow Big Sur folk and those who got lost in its mystique, as it did my family.

Ultimately, this book is a story about food, family, and the culture of place, and how it all unfolds around the table and why that matters.

My Nepenthe is also a storybook with recipes, about a third of which are memory-based, a third culled from the restaurant's archives, and the last third from when I ran Café Kevah, an outdoor café on the premises. Sprinkled throughout are recipes from family to round out the tales. Food is every part of what my family did and still does. It brings us together around the table, then and now, and all of those who grew up at Nepenthe have swirled around the kitchen and have cooked and served others at one time or another, if not still.

My Nepenthe is also very much about theatre, as restaurants tend to be, and the life and theatrical references in this book grew out of that parallel. As it was for my mother's generation, Nepenthe's terrace was our stage, where we danced and performed, often nightly. Over the years, my own kids have experienced a little of that theatre, and even today, my younger nieces, nephews, and cousins, even some visiting children, seem to understand the magic and wonder of Nepenthe right off.

And finally, this book is somewhat of a memoir, a little about me, a lot about Nepenthe and cast, and as it turned out, even more about my grandmother, Lolly, the matriarch of the Fassett family, who meant the world to me. Our family, like many other families, was messy at times, and there are many threads not told or merely written out. It is certainly not a conventional tale, but we didn't have a conventional family, something my grandparents very much celebrated. Nonetheless, Nepenthe was and is a rich legacy, and I am grateful to be a part of this crazy stew of a family. Nepenthe was always so much more than a restaurant. It had a life of its own, as my grandmother would say, and many imaginative, creative people came through its doors to help make it what it is today.

The magic and lure of Nepenthe still beckons, the buzz and whirl of the restaurant life ever bait. There is no greater haven for me. At times I long for the comfort it brings, the intimacy of early mornings when the sun peeks over the rise, the sweet sound of birds mingling with the resonance of its daily awakening, the woodiness of wintry weather and roasting marshmallows in the outdoor fireplace, the smell of fresh-baked bread permeating from the family kitchen, the beans and tomatoes simmering on the stove.

I remember my grandmother wrapping scarves around my waist and sending me down to the terrace to dance, then watching me from her windowsill. I remember escaping to the forest below the garden with its storied redwoods, bridges, and gnome-like setting; the fantastic parties, fetes, and daily happenings behind the scenes. These are just some of what I love and cherish about *my* Nepenthe, and today not only do I marvel at the stunning view, but also at the tremendous legacy my grandparents have left behind.

Cooking notes

ALL RECIPES WERE TESTED WITH A HOME GAS RANGE AND OVEN. UNLESS OTHERWISE STATED:

Eggs are large, hormone-free, and cage-free.

Chicken is natural, hormone-free.

Fish is purchased from an astute environmentally conscious purveyor.
  In Nepenthe's case, it is Kanaloa Seafood based in Santa Barbara, California.

Meats are prime.

Butter is unsalted.

Olive oil is extra virgin.

Table salt is kosher, or sometimes sea salt.

Flour is unbleached white.

Whole-wheat flour is stone-ground.

Baking powder is aluminum-free.

Fruit is seasonal, organic if possible, and preferably locally grown.

Vegetables, especially root-based, are mostly organic.

Fresh tomatoes are used only in season.

Canned tomatoes are good-quality plum tomatoes, or imported San Marzano.

The Fassett family, 1966

{ *1* }

MY FAMILY'S STORY

My family's story in Big Sur began in 1947, when my grandparents William and Madeleine Fassett, better known as Bill and Lolly, bought a rustic log cabin on a grassy knoll surrounded by oak trees and moved in with their five children: Griff, Kaffe, Dorcas Jane, Holly, and Kim, my mother, who was just nine months old.

The cabin, built in 1925 by homesteader Sam Trotter for the Trails Club, overlooks the south coast of Monterey County. Now faced by brick, for many years it was an overnight resting place for travelers and hikers and a summer retreat for club members. With its unparalleled view, it was also a favorite picnic spot for day visitors, and that was how my grandparents discovered it.

Bats and termites called the cabin home when they first saw it, and deer and rattlesnakes hovered. My grandmother refused to return until they were cleared out. Inside was a formidable wooden chest lined with tin for storing food and supplies. Right off, they added a covered porch so they could remove raingear and heavy coats before entering the cabin. Soon after, my grandmother planted a grapevine that continues to trail up the front arbor. She also made plans to add rooms on the western slope, enlisting her dear friend, the artist Douglas Madsen, to help. My grandfather, meanwhile, took jobs on the highway and in construction. The creation of Nepenthe Restaurant, a poet's paradise carved from the hillside and formed to be one with land and sea, would follow.

My grandfather's initial idea was to offer no more than a roadside stand selling hot dogs and coffee. Ultimately, he got more than he bargained for. Aesthetics aside, he wanted to create a successful enterprise and in that way got it right. A compelling storyteller, he had a way with people that drew in crowds from the start. Captivated by his tales and the unique setting, people came from all over to visit *his* Nepenthe.

My grandmother, on the other hand, had a vivid imagination and wouldn't settle for anything less than remarkable. Where my grandfather saw a hot dog stand, she looked to the piazzas of Rome and Capri of her youth, to the sun-splashed terraces of Greece, and to fellow artists and designers for inspiration. With an abiding appreciation for art and beauty and her own creative flair, she rallied for the extraordinary.

Bill and Lolly's ideals were not as far apart as they may seem, and it was their unique perspectives that ushered Nepenthe into existence. Each was necessary for the other, and Nepenthe would not be what it is today without their individual contributions. Likewise, their family histories and collective stories bring much to the making and understanding of Nepenthe's development, and similarly shed light on their distinctive personalities.

*We used to lie on the grassy slope & plan—
Bill had been trying to puzzle out how we
would survive living in the country.*

—LOLLY FASSETT

The Fassett family, 1947

Painting by Jane Powers

MY GRANDMOTHER, LOLLY FASSETT

Madeleine Adams (later known as Lolly) Ulman had what seemed like a storybook childhood. Born June 16, 1911 to Grace Madeleine Powers and Seth Ulman, she was the eldest grandchild of prominent San Francisco attorney Frank Hubbard Powers, founder of the seaside village of Carmel. She remembered him as an avid outdoorsman who took her on rambling trips as a young child over the old county road to his favorite picnic spots in Big Sur. One spot was the beach below what would become Nepenthe, where they brought fresh-picked corn from Molera Ranch and roasted it over "a glorious beach fire," staying long into the evening on moonlit nights. "When we bought the Log House thirty some odd years ago I did not realize that we were above that beach," she wrote in her notebook.

Elizabeth and Lolly

Her grandmother was the painter Jane Gallatin Powers, daughter of Albert Gallatin, a successful businessman who built for his family what is now the historic California Governor's Mansion in Sacramento, where Jane grew up from the age of nine. Lolly grew up in the Powers' family residence on Steiner Street in San Francisco with her two siblings, Elizabeth and Seth, and spent holidays and summers in Carmel, the celebrated artist colony founded by her grandfather.

In 1920, after the sudden death of her husband, Lolly's grandmother Jane moved to Europe with her three youngest children, leaving Lolly's mother in the family residence with her children. Both of Jane's younger daughters married, one to Marino Dusmet de Smours, the son of a Neapolitan duke and himself the governor of Capri, the picturesque island where my grandmother would later spend her formative years and draw inspiration for Nepenthe. Jane's son, Gallatin Powers, my grandmother's uncle, later returned to Carmel and opened two fabled restaurants, the Crocodile's Tail at Bixby Bridge and Gallatin's Restaurant in the historic Stokes Adobe in old Monterey (now a restaurant of the same name).

Frank Powers and Jane Gallatin Powers

founders of Carmel's art community

*L*olly's maternal grandfather, Frank Powers, first came to the Carmel area around 1900 after trading legal services for a plot of land. The property, at the north boundary of present-day Carmel, had sweeping views of fifteen-foot-high sand dunes leading down to the beach.

Jane Powers

Frank fell in love with the landscape and returned to live with Lolly's grandmother, the painter Jane Powers, and their four children. They moved into a board and batten ranch house on the property, later plastered it to keep out the sand, and turned an old barn into an art studio, naming their new home The Dunes.

Along with business partner Frank Devendorf, Powers started the Carmel Development Company. In 1902 he filed the first subdivision map of the village that became Carmel-by-the-Sea. Aspiring to live in a community that esteemed the arts, Frank and Jane nurtured Carmel's creative beginnings, inviting artists, writers, musicians, and poets to move there. According to family lore, Frank insisted on selling them lots for as little as $5 and $10 because he valued the way they made their livelihood. Painter William Merritt Chase, poet George Sterling, and writer Mary Austin were some of the first to take him up on his offer.

Meanwhile, Jane set up home in their rustic cabin, embellishing it with fine rugs and at one time with more than twenty chandeliers, in keeping with her former lifestyle. She helped start the Arts and Crafts Club and invited artist William Chase to give plein-air painting sessions on the beach near their home. Together she and her husband established Carmel's outdoor theatre and helped build the town's first library.

The property went down to the beach. There used to be marvelous picnics days into the night.

—LOLLY

Frank Powers, his daughter Madeleine, and Lolly

Date May 3rd Place Atlantic Ocean

The Feltre's Swimming (Pool)
Ballad.

The Feltre had a Swimming-pool,
The Boatswain fixed the hose, as a rule.
The Ocean came in so nice and cool,
And filled the Feltre's Swimming-pool.

One morning through the water-hose,
Her skin as tender as a rose,
In came a Sirene, dressed in mol,
Splashing and smashing the swimming-pool.

She came through the hose, she swung through...
She jumped in and out (she was beyond that).
Nobody saw her. At five, as a rule,
It's dark in and outside the Swimming...

apri - Faraglioni

The Barefoot Contessa

I can't help but make the comparison between Big Sur and the island of Capri, Italy, two idealized settings isolated from the daily distractions of the modern world, both dream-like destinations with bohemian roots, different but not so far apart. Big Sur's rugged coastline parallels the Amalfi coast, reaching from the peninsula of Sorrento to Salerno, with its exquisite beauty, harrowing road, and cliffside dwellings. A short distance by boat is Capri, across the Bay of Naples, and within view on a clear day. And then there is Nepenthe, perched on a cliff in California, overlooking the sea, an island unto itself.

My grandmother lived on Capri as a young woman, moving there at the impressionable age of seventeen. She arrived first at Naples by ship after forty-eight days at sea, her aunt Polly and uncle Marino Dusmet de Smours, the *podesta* (or governor) of the island, greeting her at the dock bearing a huge bunch of yellow roses. That first night they took her to a dinner party at the old duke's villa, where she recalled almost fainting due to all the excitement, setting the stage for the amazing life that she lived there.

Spirited and warm in nature, Lolly flourished in the generous setting, falling in love with the people as they did her. On the island, she became known as the Barefoot Contessa and one of two beautiful American girls, the other being her aunt Polly. There was dancing and making fun until all hours of the night, exploring the grottoes at leisure, swimming, diving for crayfish, cooking pasta on the beach, and communing with writers and artists who did not seem to have a care in the world.

Sunday about fifty of us had been invited to tea up at Anacapri. It was packs of fun. We filled nearly all the cars in Capri and sang songs all the way up. We ate all kinds of food and danced out in the open. It was a marvelous night and hearing all the lovely Neapolitan songs all the way down to Capri was enough to make anyone's heart stand still.

—LOLLY, IN A LETTER TO HER MOTHER FROM CAPRI

Her life swirled with dignitaries and heads of state. She met several times with the crown prince, Umberto di Savoia, and other members of the royal family, including Her Royal Highness the Princess Mafalda, later killed at the Buchenwald concentration camp during the war. Legend has it my grandmother danced with Mussolini at his private residence in Rome, although she would only smile when asked about it later.

It is no wonder that my grandmother felt at home in Big Sur, with its tragic landscape and budding romance with bohemian culture. The spirited and carefree lifestyle on the coast undoubtedly attracted her and stirred her already vibrant imagination. As a young girl she picnicked with her grandfather on the beach just below the old Trails Club cabin (where Nepenthe sits today) and wrote gaily about those early experiences. Here she enveloped her story in an equally magnificent setting, one that similarly attracted writers, painters, poets, and other blithe souls into its fold.

3 pounds ripe heirloom tomatoes,
    in assorted shapes, colors, and sizes
1 pound fresh mozzarella
1 handful young arugula leaves
1 handful basil leaves, preferably the smaller variety,
    left whole or torn
Pinch freshly dried oregano or marjoram (optional)
Coarse sea salt
Extra virgin olive oil
Freshly ground black pepper

Heirloom Tomato Salad with Fresh Mozzarella

La Caprese, the summer salad of tomato, mozzarella, and basil, hails from the idyllic island of Capri. In the 1950s, the Trattoria da Vincenzo, a restaurant owned by the Cosentino family, friends of my grandmother's aunt and uncle, served it as a light summer lunch for the ladies. While everyone else feasted on the rich food, the ladies would ask for a just-picked ripe tomato and fresh, locally made fior di latte, *cow's milk mozzarella. The salad usually includes a few leaves of* rughetta, *similar to arugula, and a smattering of dried wild oregano, both island grown. This recipe is adapted from one by Titina Vuotto, daughter of the Cosentinos.*

Slice the larger tomatoes into thick rounds, and the smaller ones into halves or quarters. Arrange on a large plate or platter. Gently tear the mozzarella into pieces and place on top of the tomatoes. Scatter the salad with the arugula and basil and sprinkle with the oregano and salt. Drizzle with olive oil and grind black pepper over the top. Serve immediately.

6 ounces fine-quality
  (52 to 70 percent cacao) dark chocolate
1½ cups whole almonds with skins
1 cup granulated sugar
5 eggs, separated
2 teaspoons finely grated orange zest
1 teaspoon pure vanilla extract
14 tablespoons (1¾ sticks) butter,
  melted and cooled
Pinch salt
Whipped cream

Torta Caprese (Chocolate Almond Torte from Capri)

This famous cake from Capri is made with ground whole almonds and chopped chocolate. This recipe is adapted from one a Russian cook gave to Margherita Cosentino, a friend to my grandmother's aunt Polly. Hers was made with olive oil.

Dust the torte lightly with a little confectioners' sugar or unsweetened cocoa, and serve with a dollop of fresh cream.

Preheat oven to 350°F. Lightly butter a 9-inch round baking pan, then line the bottom with parchment paper and butter the paper.

In a food processor, or using a large knife, coarsely chop the chocolate and transfer to a bowl. Finely grind the almonds with 2 tablespoons of the sugar, leaving some texture (it shouldn't be like meal). Add to the chocolate.

In the bowl of an electric mixer, beat the yolks with the remaining sugar until pale yellow and fluffy, about 5 minutes. Beat in the orange zest and vanilla. Slowly add the melted butter and beat for 30 seconds to combine. Add the chocolate and almonds and mix well.

In another bowl, beat the egg whites with the salt until they hold firm, but not stiff, peaks. Fold a third of the egg whites into the batter to lighten, and then fold in the rest.

Pour the batter into the prepared pan. Bake for 45 to 50 minutes, until the torte just begins to pull away from the side and a toothpick inserted in the center comes out relatively clean. It will still be moist. Cool on a rack for 10 minutes, then invert onto another rack, peel off the paper, and invert back onto a plate. Cool completely.

Lolly and Bill on their wedding day, 1935

MY GRANDFATHER, BILL FASSETT

Like my grandmother, my grandfather grew up in an unconventional family with a variety of wealthy influences. He was born William Elliot Griffis (McCallie) after his maternal grandfather, William Griffis, an acclaimed orientalist, on August 22, 1911, in Chattanooga, Tennessee. His birth father, Edward Lee McCallie of the McCallie School and mother, Lillian Eyre Griffis, divorced when he was only a baby. My grandfather, early on, was called Elliot, after his uncle Elliot Griffis, the American composer.

Lillian (who later renamed herself Kevah) married millionaire Newton Crocker Fassett, an earlier flame and her husband's best friend, in an infamous double-divorce marriage ceremony in Nevada. Fassett adopted Bill and his older sister, Katie, and they took his surname. My grandfather maintained the name William Elliot Fassett throughout his lifetime.

Schooled at various boarding institutions as a young man, my grandfather attended the University of California at Los Angeles and later Cornell University, his father's and stepfather's alma mater, where he studied hotel management. He eventually moved to Laguna Beach where his sister and mother resided. He became a merchant marine, setting sail to and from San Francisco where, as one of several bachelors living in the house next door, he met my grandmother while attending a party at the Powers' Steiner Street home. They were both twenty-four years old.

Within months he took my grandmother down to meet his sister, Katie, in Laguna Beach (his mother died suddenly in 1934). They planned to elope but Lolly's mother got wind of it and made haste, sending a telegram the next day. "Stop the wedding, I'm on my way," it read. They married a few days later in a small chapel across from Mission San Juan Capistrano, with Bill's very pregnant sister and her husband as witnesses. When they emerged from the chapel, the workers threw rice on Katie rather than my grandmother, thinking surely she was a shotgun bride.

My grandparents lived briefly on the cliffs of Laguna Beach. They eventually moved to the Powers family home in San Francisco, by then with two young boys, Griff and Kaffe. My grandfather worked various jobs, including at a newspaper, and palled around with the writer Herb Caen, who later wrote about Nepenthe in his column. They moved to Carmel in the early 1940s with two more children, Dorcas Jane and Holly, and lived in a "marvelous old Spanish style house with a huge living room and fireplace," according to my grandmother's letters.

An aspiring writer, my grandfather ran a magazine called *What's Doing* but gave it up when they moved to Big Sur in 1947. To sustain the family while building Nepenthe, my grandfather worked for the Trotter brothers doing construction, though it apparently didn't suit him. I was told he once backed a tractor off the cliff because he tried to read and drive at the same time.

Kevah Griffis feminist and astrologist

Bill's mother, Lillian Griffis, had an illustrious history as a proponent of birth control and astrologer to the stars. Daughter of acclaimed orientalist and author William Elliot Griffis, who was twice decorated by a Japanese emperor with the Order of the Rising Sun, Lillian was a "one of a kind soldier in the movement of women's rights," said her granddaughter Gretchen McCausland.

William, Kevah, and Katie

During her marriage to Newton Fassett she fought alongside Margaret Sanger, founder of Planned Parenthood, attending trials and marches in New York and Washington as the secretary of the Spokane Birth Control League. Educated at Vassar, Lillian pursued the political and social engagements of her day, striking out on a decidedly bohemian trail despite her status as a noted socialite. She regularly attended the more colorful salons in New York, at times taking her children along (Bill's sister, Katie, told stories about rolling condoms for distribution as a young girl).

After divorcing Fassett, Lillian married Russell Iredell, a Hollywood portraitist, and adopted the name Kevah. The spelling was connected to numerology, with the letter "H" said to symbolize the perfect balance between male and female. While Russell painted, she gave readings to the stars, wrote articles for the *New York World* and other publications, and authored a column called "Kevahgrams." As with many in her circle, she studied the teachings of G. I. Gurdjieff, an Armenian-Greek mystic who stressed self-awareness. Kevah and Russell had one son, David.

My grandfather worshipped his mother, often praising her involvement with Sanger and the "movement" and alluding to her interest in astrology and mysticism (and later his own). In 1992 we christened the café at Nepenthe in my great-grandmother's honor.

William Stanton Griffis

Bill's uncle, Stanton Griffis, was a gentleman farmer, businessman, and ambassador to Franco's Spain, Poland, Argentina, and Egypt under President Truman. He helped fund Nepenthe, showing up with wads of cash at just the right time. Evidently he had a penchant for bailing out businesses, including Paramount Pictures in the 1930s, making him a partner and linking my grandfather, and later Nepenthe, to the Hollywood scene.

EARLY DAYS IN BIG SUR

There was no electricity when my grandparents moved to Big Sur in the 1940s, and even with the opening of Highway 1 ten years earlier, the remote coastal community remained a quiet hamlet, with at most 300 full-time residents. They were a sturdy mix of ranchers, artists, bohemians, affluent retirees, business owners, descendents of pioneer families, Mexican Californians, and the region's native people.

Tourism was seasonal, leaving the land and highway to the locals from late fall to early spring. The community maintained a fierce intellectual and artistic independence, relying on the fortitude and good nature of its residents. They appreciated the isolation and inspiration found in their homeland, sharing resources and information—they sent messages, notes, and goods to their mountain neighbors via the trusty mailman, and they assembled as needed to raise a friend's barn.

With their creative resourcefulness and unconventional upbringings, my grandparents Bill and Lolly fit right in, forging alliances and friends across the spectrum and becoming an essential part of the growing community. They started building Nepenthe within the first year and, like many on the coast, determined their livelihood through hard work and enormous sacrifice.

Big Sur felt extremely remote when my family arrived, but it quickly began to change. By the mid-1950s, with an influx of tourists and "progress" arriving, the off-season months afforded a return to a simpler life, more time for family, barn dances, theatrical revues at the community Grange Hall, and potluck dinners. Then and now, social events in Big Sur often centered around food.

During low tide, the Trotter family took the Fassett kids to gather abalone, and back home they'd sit out on the porch cleaning and pounding it. "They were black abalone," said my uncle Griff, who fondly recalls those excursions. "We scooped them out of the shell, sliced them, and cooked them. You had to go in extremely low tide, early in the morning. It was very hard."

The family took to the natural rhythm of coastal life. They took long walks on the beach looking for driftwood or rambles into the hills for other treasures—roots of trees or unusual stones that my grandmother collected. She would say, "I have a brainstorm," and off they went, said my aunt Dorcas. Sometimes they'd go to Lighthouse Beach to pick up shells and skulls. My aunt recalls that her mother always made a big pot of soup beforehand, "enough for the whole town," that would be ready when they returned, as well as large batches of peanut butter cookies.

2 tablespoons olive oil, plus more for drizzling
1 medium onion, diced
2 stalks celery, diced
2 carrots, peeled and diced
1 clove garlic, minced
2 sprigs fresh thyme, stemmed
2 large ribs chard, washed, stems removed,
  and leaves cut into thin ribbons
1 potato, scrubbed and diced
1 cup cooked white beans, or 1 (15-ounce) can
  cannellini beans, drained of liquid and rinsed
2 Roma or plum tomatoes, peeled and coarsely chopped, or
  ½ (14.5-ounce) can whole plum tomatoes with some juice
6 or 7 cups vegetable stock or water
1 medium zucchini, diced
½ cup dried shell pasta or other small shaped pasta
2 or 3 tablespoons chopped fresh parsley
Salt and freshly ground black pepper
Parmesan cheese

Day at the Beach Minestrone Soup

This is a rustic, homey soup. Feel free to add different vegetables, depending on the season, like young green beans in the spring instead of chard, or butternut squash in fall and winter—as my grandmother might have done. Her tricks for a flavorful soup included adding V8 juice in place of some of the stock or water and throwing in the scrap ends of meat cooked for the restaurant. As this soup is always thicker the next day, thin with a little stock or more V8.

Heat the olive oil over medium heat in a large pot. Add the onion and cook, stirring occasionally, until translucent, about 5 minutes. Stir in the celery, carrots, garlic, and thyme; cook 2 to 3 minutes. Stir in the chard, potato, beans, tomatoes, and 6 cups stock, adding more as needed. If using canned whole tomatoes, gently crush them by pressing against the side of the pot with a wooden spoon.

Bring the soup to a boil then decrease the heat and simmer for about 25 minutes, until the vegetables are just tender. As the soup cooks, mash some of the potato with your spoon to help thicken it.

Add the zucchini and stir in the pasta. Simmer for 10 to 15 minutes, until the pasta is cooked and the flavors meld. Add the parsley and season to taste with salt and pepper. Ladle the soup into bowls. Drizzle with olive oil and grate Parmesan over the top.

½ cup (1 stick) butter, room temperature
½ cup natural peanut butter
½ cup granulated sugar
½ cup firmly packed brown sugar
1 egg
1¼ cups flour
½ teaspoon baking soda
¾ teaspoon baking powder
¼ teaspoon salt

Peanut Butter Cookies

My grandmother often made large batches of cookies for family and crew, a practice that continues to this day. My aunt Holly always has a jar of homemade cookies on her counter; this is her recipe.

You can easily slip in some whole-wheat flour, or wheat germ, as my grandmother might have done, making them more homey tasting.

Combine the butter and peanut butter in a medium-size bowl and beat with a wooden spoon or electric mixer until smooth. Add the granulated and brown sugar and beat until fluffy. Add the egg and mix well. Stir in the flour, baking soda, baking powder, and salt. Cover the dough with plastic wrap and chill in the refrigerator for 30 minutes.

Preheat the oven to 350°F.

Separate the dough into balls the size of large walnuts. Place each ball of dough 3 inches apart on a lightly greased sheet pan. Gently flatten the balls twice with the tines of a fork dipped in flour, creating a crisscross pattern.

Bake for 10 to 12 minutes, until golden.

MY GRANDPARENTS' LEGACY

My grandparents' Nepenthe was a vast playground of riches, with food not only part of the fabric of place but a necessary entry into the community and the way my family made a living. At the restaurant, Bill and Lolly served a very limited menu from the start: a couple of steaks and a roasted squab, a crisp salad, good bread, a plate of cheese, California wine. What more could you want, one journalist queried early on —you had it all, including the unrivaled setting.

My grandparents never dared to make much more of the food than that. Their ideals centered on place, one where people could forget their worldly cares and find heaven not through repast so much as through the entire experience. That Nepenthe was a restaurant was almost despite itself, the food not so much the point as the avenue to bring people together around the table.

My grandmother once described Nepenthe as something of a life force. As it grew it opened its arms to a large extended family of employees and friends, encompassing a gift shop and café, numerous pathways and meandering gardens, staff housing, water lines and wells, and the ever-necessary infrastructure to maintain it all. In this way it also caused many challenges for my grandparents, financially and otherwise, and was by no means always the carefree, gay haunt it became known as. It was and is hard work, and the challenges of running a business while raising a family took its toll.

But sixty years on, Nepenthe and the log cabin remain home to my family, and the restaurant continues to be a meeting place for friends and relatives, priding itself on its legacy of care and relaxed, inviting atmosphere. From a leisurely drive and a picnic at the old Trails Club, perched next to a young oak tree and with unparalleled views, came a dream, and so began Nepenthe.

Their ideals centered on place, one where people could forget their worldly cares and find heaven not through repast so much as through the entire experience.

Trails Club, 1940s

CHAPTER 2

*House of
No Sorrow*

For at Nepenthe, the House of No Sorrow, you may waltz or do the Mambo, you may sit erect or sprawl, you may wear dinner clothes or Levi's . . . you needn't even wear a tie. The one important thing the Fassetts want you to wear is a smile when you leave.

—FROM THE "HOUSE OF NO SORROW," 1953, AUTHOR UNKNOWN

{ 2 }

HOUSE OF NO SORROW

The legend of Nepenthe goes back before the restaurant opened, to 1944, when Orson Welles bought a Big Sur cabin for his celebrated bride, Rita Hayworth. The author Henry Miller, who was staying at the cabin with the novelist Lynda Sargent, evidently wrote a furious invective on fake parchment denouncing the Hollywood newcomers and cursing the cabin. But Welles and Hayworth never moved in. It sat empty until my grandparents, Bill and Lolly Fassett, acquired it in the fall of 1947.

Welles and Hayworth had decided to cash in their war bonds and took a driving trip down the coast with the actor Joseph Cotten, an old friend from the Mercury Theatre, said my grandfather. "They were just sort of meandering along the coast and they saw the side road and they drove up and saw this log cabin and fell in love with it, and made some inquiries around and found out they could buy it."

As the story goes, they gathered up the money between them, put $156 down to hold the purchase, measured the kitchen for a new stove and the windows for curtains, and then went on their way, never again to return. Within a year Welles and Hayworth divorced and later sold the cabin and property to my grandparents. "By '45, you know, they'd gotten a divorce and the property passed to Rita, and she was romancing with the Ali Khan."

The story of Welles and Hayworth at Nepenthe has as many versions as tellers. Some say the legendary actors stayed an hour, and others that they bought it sight unseen, paid for by their agent. I've heard that they slept only one night or none at all. On any given afternoon you can overhear guests spinning the tale to bewildered newcomers, pointing to what they believe is Welles and Hayworth's lovesick cabin just above the terrace. Rumor has it that Hayworth actually stopped at Nepenthe

years later, but Welles never did. I once read a satirical interview where Welles called Nepenthe an "opiate's dream" carved from the cliffs. Herb Caen, the San Francisco columnist, wrote in the 1950s that Welles said Hayworth "had absolutely no feel for the primitive life," and so it was.

For years, a signed photo of Rita in a sultry Hollywood pose hung in the office, inviting further romance. A zealous employee forged her signature on it in jest. Perpetuating the legend, in the early 1980s another keen employee wrote Rita's name in a newly poured section of concrete on the back veranda. For his "Love, Rita" he lost his job. But in typical Nepenthe fashion then, he was rehired the next day.

THE RESTAURANT'S CREATION

My grandmother wanted to build cabins on the hillside and rent them out. My grandfather wanted to build a stand on the side of the road to sell coffee and burgers and call it Bill's Place. Both ideas met with resistance. The cabins were later built, but as staff housing.

"I thought I'd have a little stand on the highway and sell frozen orange juice and hot dogs, but the neighbors put the kaibash on that," my grandfather recalled in one of many interviews. "Within three days so many people dropped in on us, I told my wife, 'Honey, we ought to start a restaurant.' We did and started to charge money for food. This cost us our friends, but since then we have won many new ones."

They decided to build a place up on the hill with the view, and thus began Nepenthe. My grandfather often joked about Nepenthe's unlikely beginnings, and later marveled at what it had become. My grandmother maintained that the land and encompassing view were too beautiful to keep to themselves and must be shared with the world, eventually articulating that sentiment and printing it on the back of the menu. She had an enduring understanding and appreciation for Big Sur and its people, and felt strongly that Nepenthe belonged to everyone.

After a series of architects proposed ideas for a restaurant, my grandparents met Rowan Maiden, a former student of Frank Lloyd Wright, and felt he shared in their enthusiasm for the site and overall project, so they commissioned him to develop their plans. My grandmother imagined an open-air pavilion for good food, dancing, and Sunday afternoon concerts, a place for people to come and forget their worldly cares. She worked closely with Maiden to achieve her ideas.

Maiden designed the building to take advantage of the view and light patterns, paying close attention to the surrounding geography and the original cabin. Final plans called for a semicircular terrace facing south and a 100-foot bench running the length of the restaurant. A contemporary kitchen along the interior wall attached to a semicircular bar (later expanded to a full circle) and an open fireplace in the center of the room advanced the design. The cost of building rose to $22,000 from an early estimate of only $3,000.

Rowan Maiden
Architect

Raised in Piedmont, California, Rowan Maiden attended the UC Berkeley School of Architecture in the 1930s. In 1939 he joined the Frank Lloyd Wright Taliesin Fellowship at its winter camp in Arizona, where he lived for three years, migrating between Arizona and Spring Green, Wisconsin, its summer campus. There, Rowan met Germaine Schneider, whose father helped design and plant Taliesin's first domestic garden, and they soon married.

In 1946, they moved to Monterey in an area called Huckleberry Hill, a community of artists and writers, among them Bruce Ariss, a contemporary of John Steinbeck. During this period, Rowan met my grandparents and won the commission to design Nepenthe, his best-known project. He died in 1957 after falling from a barn roof in Big Sur. Rowan and Germaine had three children; his daughter Romney, since passed, is my namesake.

Frank Lloyd Wright, who didn't believe in making architects so much as he did master builders of both intellect and creativity, was said to have regretted losing only three apprentices over the years, and Rowan was one of them.

Nepenthe was unique and didn't follow any particular style trends. It is a very strong building, unique in many ways.

—HENRIK BULL, ARCHITECT

My grandmother wanted a big, open room without posts. Maiden came up with the idea of using trusses that fit together like a "giant jigsaw puzzle." It took twelve men to put one of them up. Big Sur builder Frank Trotter, who my grandmother believed "had a solution for everything," figured out how to make it work. They even employed a shipwright to make some of the sections.

Brothers Frank and Walter Trotter, known for their massive strength and hearty appetites, built the structure using native materials and hand-hewn redwood from the canyons. They poured red concrete for the terrace and embedded redwood discs around the old oak tree to mark the entrance. (The inlaid chessboard did not appear until the early 1960s.)

Soon they were "baking bricks," as my grandmother put it, using decomposed granite, cement, and fire clay for the outdoor fireplace. She spearheaded its construction between changing diapers and feeding the crew. "She was the straw-boss directing us all," remembers my uncle Griff of his mother and her two friends that helped. "These Amazon women and myself, mixing concrete and pouring forms." They used local gravel from the mountainside and ZEV, an artist friend, made the forms. He also fashioned the original mosaics inside and around the outdoor fireplace using shards of glass, beads, tesserae, coins, and pebbles.

My grandmother collected old boards, driftwood, and other found objects for building projects. Her ability to create something out of little reflected her sense of economy and became her signature style, whether it was in remodeling or throwing together a pot of soup, or a large batch of hotcakes. Even Walter Trotter, who for all his rough veneer had a soft and generous side, saved old boards for her and brought her unusual pieces of wood he found on the beach— "driftwood he knew she would understand and love," my uncle Kaffe recalled. For the children's rooms on the west-facing slope of the property,

later staff housing, she scavenged boards from the recently demolished military barracks at Fort Ord. She put her kids to work pulling out the nails, instructing them to set aside the straight ones to reuse, a job my aunt Holly said they all loathed.

Nepenthe's modern design garnered considerable attention before and for years after its opening. In 1950, both *Architectural Forum* and *Arts & Architecture*, two respected architectural magazines, featured Nepenthe's design with photos by renowned California photographer Morley Baer, giving it exposure at the beginning and drawing interest from around the world. A German magazine apparently awarded Nepenthe a prize for showcasing a classic example of a small business in America.

Opening Day of Nepenthe

*N*epenthe derives from the Greek and means "no sorrow." In myth,
the wife of Thonis, king of Egypt, gave the drug called nepenthe to Helen,
daughter of Jove, to induce forgetfulness and surcease sorrow.
The word and concept is used throughout literature to reflect a feeling of
timelessness, and symbolizes the spirit of my grandparents' vision to
create an "isle of no-care." Homer refers to nepenthe in the Odyssey
and Poe in his poem "The Raven":
Quaff, oh quaff this kind Nepenthe
And forget this lost Lenore.

OPENING DAY

Nepenthe opened its doors on the afternoon of April 24, 1949, just over a year after breaking ground. My grandparents threw a smashing opening day party. Some 500 guests showed up, with a smattering of artists and writers, setting the stage for a lively artistic following. They included the photographer Cole Weston and his family from Carmel, and Dr. Eric Berne, creator of Transactional Analysis and the author of *Games People Play*. *Life* magazine's San Francisco bureau chief arrived hoping to catch sight of authors Henry Miller and John Steinbeck, who were rumored to attend, but Miller skipped the festivities and took all the kids to the beach. Steinbeck, alas, didn't show.

A "genuine social and artistic event," wrote the magazine *What's Doing*, of opening day. "Solid citizens, bankers, ranchers, real estate men and women mingled freely with sandaled and jeaned and corduroy shirted writers and painters and musicians and sculptors who took a few hours away from work to wish the Fassetts well on their opening day." The magazine claimed the group of well-wishers was the most "interestingly mixed group of people ever to grace the Peninsula."

Frank and Walter Trotter were bouncers and greeters for the event. An old friend, Englishman Peter King Monk, who eventually returned to work at Nepenthe, arrived at Nepenthe unwittingly that day. Not ones to mince words, the impressively sized Trotter brothers told him, "Learn how to drink beer now, because by the time the weekend is over, they won't have any."

Walter and Frank Trotter

Nepenthe served a buffet menu that included watercress sandwiches on white bread and smoky teas, but forgot to charge half the people. The mood was festive and the party lasted through the evening. Poet James Broughton read his award-winning book-length play, *The Playground*, and followed with a book signing. Music and folk dancing created a scene that became synonymous with Nepenthe in the years after.

ZEV a Nepenthe artist

Z**EV's** artistic handprint is evident throughout Nepenthe. Born Daniel Harris, he later adopted the name "ZEV," meaning "wolf" in Hungarian. A prolific artist who showed work at museums and galleries across the world, he contributed illustrations to James Broughton's *The Playground*, read on Nepenthe's opening day. He was behind the fantastical naming of menu items and encouraged the mythical fairy-tale-like setting. ZEV created the whimsical bird logo and constructed mosaics inside and outside the restaurant, as well as contributed drawings and ideas to many print ads for Nepenthe.

Sculptor Harry Dick Ross and Kim, my mother

NEPENTHE'S EARLY YEARS

Before electricity arrived, my grandfather installed an old army surplus generator that they ran for an hour each night for radio and reading. Other times they used kerosene lamps, lit the restaurant solely with candles, and cooked on a gas grill. The refrigerator man arrived once a week with a huge block of ice that he transferred to a wooden cupboard with tongs.

When the restaurant opened, my grandfather bartended, my grandmother cooked and served, and all the kids helped. There was never a shortage of work, from stacking firewood or de-nailing boards, to setting up and closing down the restaurant (which included cleaning the candle wax from the brass holders nightly), to bussing tables (my grandfather made the kids pay for anything they broke), chopping carrots, slicing pickles, and sitting "knee to knee" out on the back porch, peeling potatoes for french fries.

Uncle Griff, who was ten years old when they moved to Big Sur, worked as a dishwasher and on the clean-up crew. One spring he cooked, and later he kept that job through college.

Uncle Kaffe became the first busboy. He spilled wine at a drunken couple's table once and quickly nabbed a dark cloth to mop it up, realizing too late it was the woman's black lace glove. The husband, seeing his shame, pressed a $5 bill into his hand and sent him on his way. He did better on the artistic front, making cards and drawings and selling them from a small orange crate store he set up in the parking lot. He also tended a vegetable garden on the side of the hill, taught folk dance and led his siblings in theatrical performances, participated in the fashion shows, and painted, setting up elaborate still life displays and employing his siblings as models.

Just after closing each fall, my grandfather took a group of friends on an annual hike, taking two to three days, over the hills to the hot springs near Tassajara, not yet a Zen center then. He filled his backpack with bottles of wine and books, and everyone was rip-roaring drunk by noon, remembered Clovis Harrod who went one year. Others recalled the extraordinary discussions around the fire pit, where my grandfather also read aloud from his favorite books. He took these trips throughout the mid-1970s, and they were occasionally written about in the newspaper.

Aunt Dorcas also excelled in the arts and was a natural performer. She studied flamenco with a visiting dance troupe that stayed on with the family for many months, mastering castanets and later becoming a belly dancer. Like her older brothers, Dorcas helped with the various jobs necessary to run the restaurant, from splitting logs to making fires and doing clean-up detail. Although she professes not to be much of a cook, she created the first Crab Louis for the restaurant and made her special orange chiffon cake with orange liqueur for Sunday brunch.

Aunt Holly and my mother, Kim, also participated when they were younger. By age twelve, my mother was a salad chef and cook. Even though she was barely tall enough to see over the counter, she was slinging burgers and serving sandwiches

on weekend days. As a budding teen, Holly spent one very homesick year in New York with my grandfather's family. She returned home, never to leave again. She waited on tables when she turned twenty-one, and by the mid-1970s became the manager, taking business courses and educating herself as she went along, as well as becoming a master knitter and excellent baker. Today she runs Nepenthe with her son, Kirk.

My grandfather, wanting to bring culture to the children and to Big Sur, brought string quartets from San Francisco to play on Sundays. They were huge events, covered by the *San Francisco Chronicle*, which said, "The musical reward for such a pilgrimage could not be surpassed, anywhere." He offered poets a stage to give readings, a place for lecturers to speak and give slide shows, and filmmakers to show their films as well as other musical offerings. My grandfather had "an amazing capacity for reaching out to people and getting them there," said Bill Stewart, a long-time Carmel attorney and friend. Many of the artists and creative people left behind lengthy careers elsewhere and reinvented themselves, and Nepenthe and the children provided a ready muse for their artistic imaginations.

What happened at Nepenthe was in the epiphanous stage. The musicians were performing and staging the music of their lives in the full range of that potential. Things happened that were really transcendent. Magic happened, at times, through the music.

—GRIFF FASSETT

Dorcas, late 1960s

MAKES 1 CAKE, SERVING 10 TO 12

CHIFFON CAKE
2 cups cake flour
1½ cups granulated sugar
2 teaspoons baking powder
½ teaspoon salt
6 eggs, separated, plus 1 egg white
½ cup vegetable oil
Zest and juice of 2 oranges (juice should equal ¾ cup;
  add water if necessary)
2 tablespoons Grand Marnier
¾ teaspoon cream of tartar

SIMPLE ORANGE GLAZE
2 tablespoons butter, softened
1 cup confectioners' sugar, sifted
2 teaspoons fresh orange juice
1 teaspoon hot water
1 teaspoon orange zest
½ teaspoon pure vanilla extract or Grand Marnier

Orange Chiffon Cake

Considered the "cake discovery of the century," the chiffon cake became a marketing phenomenon around the time Nepenthe opened, with recipes appearing weekly in newspapers across the country and on the back of the Softasilk cake flour box.

My aunt Dorcas made her version with orange juice and Grand Marnier for Nepenthe's Sunday brunch. This version is light and fluffy with a distinctly orange taste. To serve, top with orange glaze or simply dust with confectioners' sugar.

Preheat the oven to 325°F. Have ready a 10-inch tube cake pan, preferably with a removable bottom. Do not grease or flour it.

For the cake, sift the flour, 1⅓ cups of the granulated sugar, the baking powder, and salt into a large bowl. Whisk the egg yolks with the oil in a medium bowl. Make a well in the dry ingredients and stir in the wet ingredients. Stir in the zest, juice, and Grand Marnier.

In a large, clean bowl, beat all the egg whites until frothy. Add the cream of tartar and remaining granulated sugar, and beat until stiff, but not dry, peaks form. Fold the whites into the batter until just blended.

Scrape the batter into the ungreased cake pan. Bake for 50 to 60 minutes, until the cake springs back to the touch. Immediately turn the cake over onto the neck of a bottle and let sit, undisturbed, until completely cool (at least 1½ hours) before removing from the pan.

For the glaze, cream the butter in a small bowl using a wooden spoon. Add the confectioners' sugar, alternating with the juice and water. Beat until smooth. Stir in the orange zest and vanilla. The glaze should be thin enough to drizzle. If not, thin with a drop or two of hot water.

When the cake is cool, spread the top with the glaze, allowing it to drip down the sides.

NEPENTHE

After the restaurant opened, watching through the cabin windows at the scene below became our favorite pastime. It was our TV. We'd lay on the long row of beds in the cabin and watch. Once someone sent a box of shiny red apples to the cabin, saying it was for all the little faces in the window.

—HOLLY FASSETT

SERVES 4

DRESSING
¼ cup mayonnaise
1 tablespoon minced green pepper
1 tablespoon minced green onion or chives
½ teaspoon prepared horseradish, or ¼ teaspoon hot mustard
2 tablespoons fresh lemon juice
2 tablespoons heavy cream
Chile sauce
1 tablespoon chopped fresh parsley, fresh tarragon, or a mix
Salt and freshly ground black pepper

SALAD
1 head butter lettuce, leaves separated, rinsed, and thoroughly dried
2 heaping cups fresh crabmeat, preferably Dungeness
      (or a mix of crab and bay shrimp)
1 avocado, halved, pitted, and cut into large dice
4 radishes, thinly sliced
2 eggs, hard-cooked, peeled, and quartered
1 lemon, cut into wedges
Fresh parsley or chopped chives, for garnish

Dungeness Crab Louis Salad

*A West Coast invention, Crab Louis arrived on the restaurant scene after the turn of the
20th century and became popular again in the 1950s when we started to serve it. Make
it on one of those crisp but sunny California winter days when the Dungeness season is
on. Pick up two freshly cooked crabs (you'll need at least 2 cups lump meat) and ask the
fishmonger to crack them for you.*

To make the dressing, mix the mayonnaise, green pepper, onion, and horseradish in a
bowl. Whisk in the lemon juice and cream. Add a dash of chile sauce (or to taste), stir
in the parsley, and season with salt and black pepper. To thin, stir in 2 teaspoons water.

To make the salad, arrange the larger outer leaves of the lettuce on 4 chilled plates so
that they create loose bowl shapes to hold the chopped salad. Thinly slice the inner
leaves and arrange in mounds at the centers.

Lightly dress the crabmeat with a spoonful or two of the dressing, just enough to
moisten, and season with salt and pepper. Spoon heaping rounds of crab on the
lettuce mounds. Divide the avocado and radishes among the salads, scattering them
in a pretty fashion, and tuck in the egg quarters. Drizzle the salads with the remaining
dressing and garnish with lemon wedges and just a pinch of parsley to finish.

2 ounces heavy cream
1½ ounces gin
1 whole egg, chilled
1 tablespoon granulated sugar
Splash of sweet and sour mix
Splash of Grand Marnier
Nutmeg

George's Famous Ramos Fizz

Combine the cream, gin, egg,
sugar, sweet and sour mix, and
Grand Marnier in a blender
and whirl until frothy, about
30 seconds. Pour into a tall
glass. Grate fresh nutmeg
over top.

THE SCENE

At its start, Nepenthe opened for dinner Tuesdays through Saturdays, and at noon on Sundays to include brunch, then closed at midnight. Initially the restaurant stayed open until 2:00 a.m. on weekend nights, but after a fatal car crash involving a guest, my grandparents decided to close earlier, and the restaurant has adhered to that ever since. Into the mid-1960s, the restaurant closed for the season on November 1, following a masked ball at Halloween, a wild event that continues to this day as a benefit for the Big Sur Volunteer Fire Brigade. It reopened on April 1, following a practice dinner where the new staff waited on the returning staff.

Many of the staff headed to Mexico or other parts during the break. Our original wait team of Bill Worth and Guy Lawlor saved up enough money to buy a dude ranch in Northern California, spending the off months there and resuming in season at Nepenthe for the few years after. "All the Hollywood stars dropped in," Bill said. "I remember waiting on Greer Garson, she was *so* beautiful and gracious and gave me an autograph for Willie."

By the mid-1950s Nepenthe had added lunch service, with husband and wife duo Dotty and George Lopes at the helm. They opened year-round in the late 1960s. Dotty cooked and ran the office, and George, with his waxed handlebar mustache and white pirate-style shirts and black pencil pants, poured drinks and entertained the guests.

People came just to see George and drink his special Ramos Fizz. Some made it a weekly event, hailing from Pebble Beach and as far away as San Francisco. Actor Richard Burton adored him and tried to cast him in a Salem commercial, but George protested saying, "I don't smoke Salems." Dotty had a wonderful sense of humor and a mothering presence about her, advising one waitress upon her arrival, "In Big Sur, nobody cares what you do, so long as they know about it."

An avid Ping-Pong player, my grandfather installed a game table in the restaurant during the winter months, and artists and intellectuals dropped in for the challenge, often staying late into the night. Author Henry Miller was a remarkable player but never changed his serve, costing him many a game, according to my grandmother.

Likewise, there were marathon poker games at the half-round tables in the restaurant. Even my grandmother played occasionally, along with the author Dennis Murphy and a host of friends from Carmel. When they tired they rolled out sleeping bags on the floor next to the roaring fire, and then started all over again in the morning. Aunt Holly recalled seeing someone slip money into my grandmother's brassiere one morning before school when they were all still there.

In 1959, *Life* magazine did a feature on Big Sur's "Creative Colony," including a two-page photo spread of Nepenthe's bar scene, where Henry held forth with his roster of friends, and dancers entertained on the patio.

Eric Barker, Henry Miller, Harry Dick Ross, and Giles Healey

Henry Miller

*H*enry Miller arrived penniless in Big Sur in 1944, showing up at the cabin before Orson Welles and Rita Hayworth bought it. He spent his first couple months sleeping on the floor, sharing the space with the novelist Lynda Sargent, who lived and wrote at the cabin for several years. Evidently they didn't take kindly to each other at first, but soon enough they could be found tap, tapping away far into the night on their respective typewriters.

He wrote of his situation in *Big Sur and the Oranges of Hieronymus Bosch*, "What the budding artist needs is the privilege of wrestling with his problems in solitude—and now and then a piece of red meat."

A fixture at Nepenthe in the early days, he wrote about Nepenthe and the Fassetts in that same book:

There is another family I cannot pass over without a word or two, since here, once again, the children dominate the scene. I mean the Fassett family whose abode is "Nepenthe," one of the show places along the Coast. Lolly and Bill, the parents, are busy seven months of the year running the establishment, which specializes in food, drink, and dancing. The kids—up until recently, at any rate—specialized in raising hell. All five of them . . .

The parents, of course, are sometimes puzzled by the various problems this brood presents. Particularly Bill, the provider, who, before he hit on the brilliant idea of opening "Nepenthe," used to sit up nights wondering how to feed and clothe such a tribe. But those days are past. His chief problem now is: should Griff, the oldest one, be sent to Europe to have his fling or should he be permitted to stay in Big Sur and become a Jack of all trades. The major problem is—where will they all go to live, what part of the world, when Bill has made his pile?

A rather pleasant problem, I should say. Why not Capri?

RESTAURANT LIFE

"Steak and salads" became Nepenthe's motto. A menu from the mid-1950s featured a Phoenix Special (a complete steak dinner including fries, salad, and coffee) for $3.50, an Ambrosia Burger for $.60, Golden Plumes (french fries) for $.35, and a pitcher of beer for $1.50. Many of the original menu items had unusual names or descriptions, such as Abridged Milkshakes "as thick as a dictionary" or Nectar of the Gods for coffee. An amusing list of cocktails and after-dinner drinks sold for a song.

My grandparents rejected the notion of fine dining and white tablecloth affairs, wanting a place where everyone felt welcome, a casual establishment where you "could drop in for snacks, a glass of beer, and a bit of comradeship with friends as well." Food took a backseat to the setting, but some considered it a gourmet's paradise. The cooks prepared everything fresh and from scratch. My grandmother made sure staff washed and crisped the salad greens daily and the leaves were torn, not cut.

The Tossed Green Salad with Chef's Special Dressing cost $.60 when we opened. Waiters tossed it tableside, and author Henry Miller insisted on tossing his own, causing quite a stir. A separate menu item, the Nepenthe Salad Bowl, served at dinner, called for lining a large red plastic bowl with the outer leaves of romaine, then filling with chopped lettuce, and both bean salad and coleslaw. It also cost $.60.

Being so off the beaten track and with a small staff, there were limitations to what the restaurant could do, as it remains today in some ways. Finding staff could be hard, and when they found good people, they hung on to them. In turn, my grandparents offered a ready-made family complete with kids, dogs, and dinner. You didn't just work there, but became a part of the fabric of place. "You weren't like waiters," said Helen Morgenrath, a dancer and longtime waitress throughout Nepenthe's heyday. "Lolly made you feel like you were a host."

Adding to the challenges, deliveries occurred only once a week, if that, and the selection was limited. Many items had to be picked up in town, like the rich, chocolate cake with coconut frosting from Carmel's Wishart's Bakery we served during the week. Some people just dropped by if they had something to sell, like the butcher who was also a fisherman, who brought the first salmon of the season.

I feel that being of service to your fellow man is a privilege—if someone seems difficult don't let it get to you but see it as a challenge and do the best you can. The view and the ambience usually has its impact—if given a chance—[and] that means that the one serving is gracious and should not become a part of one's discontent. Nearly everyone, including you working here, were drawn by a certain magic quality and you should really be an extension of this feeling. We want everyone who comes to Nepenthe and Big Sur to leave with a lasting memory of a beautiful experience—after all Nepenthe means "Surcease from Sorrow!"

—LOLLY

The Telephone

Opposed to the idea of telephones on the property for years ("Everybody will call to see if there was fog or not," my grandfather said), my grandparents conceded with a pay phone in the late 1950s, installing it on the ramp leading up to the restaurant. The new phone did not go unnoticed. One San Francisco columnist wrote that after eight happy years without one, they have "at last installed a telephone—a pay job down in the parking lot."

It wasn't until the mid-1960s that my grandparents installed a pay phone outside the back door of the restaurant, and even later when they acquired a phone for the restaurant, although my grandmother never allowed one in the log cabin. "Not over my dead body," she used to say. At one point an intercom phone was installed in the family kitchen, but it didn't take outside calls, nor could we make them.

My grandmother regularly fed people who couldn't pay, usually in her family kitchen. Ken Wright, a longtime Big Sur resident and former state highway patrolman, told me he always knew my grandmother's kitchen would be open for people in need. "If there was someone truly destitute, I knew I could take them up to Nepenthe and they would be given a meal," he said. "There was no stigma, it just occurred."

By the mid-1950s, steaks at Nepenthe were $5.50, although "Beer in pitchers still comes cheap enough so Big Surites can afford to come," wrote one enthusiastic reviewer. Where else can you enjoy good food amid "a picture of paganism [and] whirling fire worshippers?" he asked in 1955, "or where can you watch a decorous Adam and Eve wearing only fig leaves dance the night away on Hallows eve?"

In 1964, with the cult of coastal bohemian life well documented, the *Saturday Evening Post* gave a scathing review of Big Sur, decrying its loss of soul and accusing Nepenthe, with its $3.50 Cheddar Steak, of driving away the artists. Some people were furious, but most didn't give it credence. My grandfather, who himself had dreams of writing the "great American novel" between serving customers, dissented: "I still would like to keep it a place for the guy who is painting or writing a book: the 'bearded one,' if you will."

SERVES 1 OR 2

¾ pound lean ground beef
Salt and freshly ground black pepper
2 slices (2 ounces) Tillamook Cheddar cheese
3 green onions, white with some green parts, finely chopped

Nepenthe Ground Steak (Cheddar Steak)

Our ground steak dinner was a whopping ¾ pound of lean beef topped with melted Tillamook Cheddar cheese and showered with green onions. It was a poor man's steak, but revered nonetheless, and it stayed on our menu into the current century, until we upgraded the menu. We still have a few old-timers who ask for it. Use the best lean ground chuck, or ask the butcher to grind it from better steaks.

Heat a grill or grill pan over medium-high heat. Form the beef into a large ball. On waxed paper, pat the ball into a large oval patty, about ½ to ¾ inch thick. Season the patty on both sides with salt and pepper.

Grill the patty on the hottest part of the grill, turning once after the blood rises to the. Top with the cheese immediately after turning and cook until desired doneness, 12 to 15 minutes total for medium rare.
Top with the green onions.

The Nepenthe Grind

Nepenthe prides itself on using the finest lean beef coarsely ground especially for us. My grandmother went to the butcher and created a custom grind from different meats, and it became what is known on the Monterey Peninsula as the Nepenthe grind. For years other restaurants tried to replicate it using their own butchers. Our longtime cook and now human resources person, Willie Nelson, who started working at the restaurant as a teenager in the early 1960s, can tell the Nepenthe grind by the feel. "If your hands feel greasy when handling the meat, it is not our grind," she tells young cooks on the line today.

SERVES 4

AMBROSIA SAUCE
1 cup mayonnaise
¼ cup tomato sauce
¼ cup mild green salsa

BURGERS
1½ pounds freshly ground lean beef
4 French rolls
2 tablespoons butter, melted
4 slices Tillamook Cheddar cheese (optional)

Ambrosia Burger

Enjoying an Ambrosia Burger on the terrace with a basket of fries and a pint of dark beer is the quintessential Nepenthe experience. According to Greek mythology, ambrosia was the food of the gods, offering immortality. The early menus described the burger in keeping with the legend and my grandfather's humor: "Like a Phoenix bird's egg in a nest, it is served in a basket with shoestrings (not including the one we started on)."

The beef should be quite lean and the grind should be coarse. (I like grass-fed beef for flavor and health, though we do not use it at the restaurant.) The beef patties are grilled, then served on a toasted, buttered French roll slathered with Ambrosia Sauce. Use the extra sauce as a dip for the Golden Plumes (french fries).

For the sauce, whisk together the mayonnaise, tomato sauce, and salsa in a bowl.

Preheat the grill. For the burgers, form the meat into 4 six-ounce balls. Lay each on a piece of waxed paper and pat into rounds, about ½ inch thick. The edges should be slightly cracked and not perfectly smooth.

Slice the rolls in half lengthwise and lay face side up on a baking sheet. Brush with the melted butter. Grill the burgers over medium hot coals or an open gas flame, turning once when the blood rises to the top, until desired doneness. For a perfect medium-rare, look for clear juices rising to the surface of the cooked side, 6 to 7 minutes. Add cheese just before it is finished.

While the burger cooks, toast the rolls face side down on a preheated flat griddle or cast-iron skillet, or face up in an oven, until they are nicely toasted and brown.

Slather the rolls with Ambrosia Sauce. Place each burger on a roll, and top with the other half. Cut in half on a diagonal and serve.

SERVES 4 TO 6

4 russet potatoes, peeled
High-heat vegetable oil, such as safflower or canola
Kosher salt

Golden Plumes (French Fries)

Crisp Golden Plumes, sprinkled with salt and towered in a basket, do the trick every time, eliciting "oohs" and "aahs" from guests and calming cranky children immediately. For years we made our own fries, my mother and her siblings peeling potatoes, then pushing them through a tabletop cutter to make shoestrings. Serve with Ambrosia Sauce (page 65).

Cut the potatoes into shoestrings about ¼ inch wide. Soak the cut potatoes in cold water for 15 minutes or so, then thoroughly pat dry before frying.

Heat 1 inch of oil in a heavy large frying pan to 365°F. It should be hot enough to fry a cube of bread golden brown in less than a minute. Fry the potatoes in batches, leaving room around them, for 2 to 3 minutes, until pale golden, then transfer to a paper towel–lined tray. Repeat with the remaining potatoes. Between batches, check the oil and bring it back up to temperature as needed. If it is not hot enough, the potatoes will soak up too much oil.

When you have finished, fry the shoestrings again, cooking for 3 to 5 minutes more, or until golden brown and crisp. Transfer to a new towel-lined tray or basket and sprinkle with salt.

Cody and Djin

Chaco

Russian mercenary

Chaco lived in the little shack behind the woodshop when we were growing up. He doubled as a drink waiter and maintenance man, and always wore the same uniform—a white shirt, scarf, and beret. Evidently he escaped from Russia through Siberia after the war, passing through South America, before arriving in the States and landing at Nepenthe sometime in the 1950s. It was Chaco who created the Siberia section on the front terrace, where he peddled White Russian cocktails to guests and would fling their change over the edge if he deemed it less than satisfactory.

Every morning Chaco built the fire in the potbelly stove in the family kitchen for my grandmother and hosed down the terrace to ready it for guests. After my cousin Kirk was born, he would call up to him through the window each morning, "Kiirky, Kiirky, come down" he would say, in his thick Russian accent.

He wrote adventure stories and poems, always hoping to be published. One poem sent to my grandparents, years after he left, reminisces about their "cottage by the sea" and expresses his longing to see them again. My uncle Kaffe said Chaco used to bury clothes, food, and other items in the woods and would sometimes sell little drawings to guests, telling Kaffe that if he were to draw them, that he would sell them, and together they would make a fortune.

ROQUEFORT DRESSING
2 teaspoons granulated garlic
2 teaspoons dried basil
2 teaspoons dried oregano
2 teaspoons dried mustard
2 teaspoons coarsely ground black pepper
2 teaspoons brown sugar
1 teaspoon salt
5 to 6 ounces Roquefort cheese
⅔ cup red wine vinegar
½ cup olive oil
1 cup canola or safflower oil

CHOPPED SALAD
2 heads romaine lettuce
1 head green leaf lettuce
4 to 6 cherry tomatoes
Freshly ground black pepper

Chopped Salad with Roquefort Dressing

Nepenthe's house salad is a mixture of chopped romaine and green leaf lettuce topped with a cherry tomato and this chunky Roquefort dressing. Greens should be freshly washed and crisped in the refrigerator, then torn rather than chopped, a distinction my grandmother was adamant about. Sometimes I might look for tender hearts of romaine and leave them whole, then combine with Little Gem lettuce or butter lettuce. Use a quart-size glass jar with a tight-fitting lid to make the dressing.

For the dressing, combine the garlic, basil, oregano, mustard, pepper, sugar, and salt in a clean glass jar. Crumble the cheese and add to the jar. Add the vinegar and oils. Cover and shake vigorously until thoroughly combined. Taste and adjust seasonings if needed. You will have more than enough dressing; refrigerate any extra.

For the salad, wash and thoroughly dry the lettuces, trimming the ends and discarding any bruised leaves. Tear into bite-size pieces and place in individual chilled bowls. Top with the desired amount of dressing, making sure each salad has plenty of blue cheese chunks. Add the cherry tomatoes and grind black pepper over the tops.

A blanket of sky and sea merge on the horizon, and on a clear day there is no limit to the scenery, unspoiled and immense in nature.

SERVES 4

GORGONZOLA BUTTER
1 tablespoon olive oil
6 tablespoons butter, room temperature
1 medium yellow onion, sliced ¼ inch thick
Salt
4 ounces Gorgonzola cheese
Freshly ground black pepper

STEAKS
4 (10- to 12-ounce) New York strip steaks, room temperature
Kosher salt and freshly ground black pepper
¼ cup (½ stick) butter, melted and solids skimmed off
4 stalks curly endive (chicory), rinsed and thoroughly dried

Phoenix Special Steak

The Phoenix Steak Dinner on our original menu consisted of either a prime New York strip or filet mignon served with a stalk of endive and came with french fries, tossed green salad, and coffee for a whopping $3.50, considered expensive then. Once aged on the premises, our steaks are prime beef and grilled to medium-rare over an open flame and brushed with melted butter at the last minute to bring up the juices. We now top the steak with Gorgonzola butter and serve it with a baked potato or a tower of shoestring fries (Golden Plumes, page 66).

For the Gorgonzola butter, heat the oil and 1 tablespoon of the butter in a skillet over medium heat. Add the onion and a pinch of salt and cook, stirring occasionally, until deeply caramelized, about 30 minutes. Set aside to cool. Mix the remaining 5 tablespoons butter with the Gorgonzola cheese in a small bowl. Stir in half of the cooled onions, and reserve the other half to serve on the side. Season with salt and pepper if needed.

For the steaks, heat a grill or grill pan over medium-high heat. Shape the steaks with the palm of your hand so they are a little plumper in the center and season with salt and pepper.

Place the steaks on the hottest part of the grill and cook to desired doneness, 6 to 7 minutes per side for medium-rare, turning only once (maybe twice to get a good score on the bottom). Just before the steaks are done, brush with the melted butter.

Arrange the steaks on 4 plates with a stalk of endive and some reserved caramelized onions. Top each steak with a bit of Gorgonzola butter.

The Fassett family, 1950s

He [Bill] had a distaste for time clocks, traffic signals, crowded sidewalks and all the other things that tether a soaring spirit.

—FROM "THE HOUSE OF NO SORROW"

For all of Nepenthe's magic, running the family business created enormous challenges for my grandparents and caused a great deal of stress. Each winter, for example, they borrowed money to get them through until the season opened on April 1, leaving little extra for extravagances or travel. But that friction, as my aunt Holly pointed out, likening it to the making of a pearl, is also what made it work.

Someone who worked at the restaurant early on once told me that people chose to work for my grandmother or for my grandfather, and otherwise learned to balance the two. During difficult times, my grandmother staged her defense from her living room. Optimistic and spiritual in nature, she expended her energy on the welfare of her guests and employees, treating them more like family and believing the guests themselves were what made the place successful, a management style that had its own unique challenges and repeatedly frustrated my grandfather, though no doubt amused him as well. "Learning how to handle Lolly was a course in itself," said Peter King Monk, the Englishman who worked for my family for more than two decades. "All you had to do was be honest," he said.

My grandfather griped about the cost of food and alcohol, and the overall burden of running the place, although he was known to come through the restaurant and shout, "Get me a bottle of Courvoisier," then play dominoes with friends for the afternoon, and later complain about the liquor costs. Because of his humor and intellect, however, he maintained a large group of friends and admirers, many who came down to spend the day with him, not for the food or even the view, but to revel in his character and wit. My grandfather's way with people is what brought Peter to Nepenthe for the duration. "Nepenthe was basically the center point of Big Sur," he recalled. He said my grandfather held court at the bar, regaling people with his stories. It was all about showing them a good time, and guests lapped it up.

My grandmother once said of his dual reputation: "The artists here think of him as a businessman; the businessmen in town think of him as an artist."

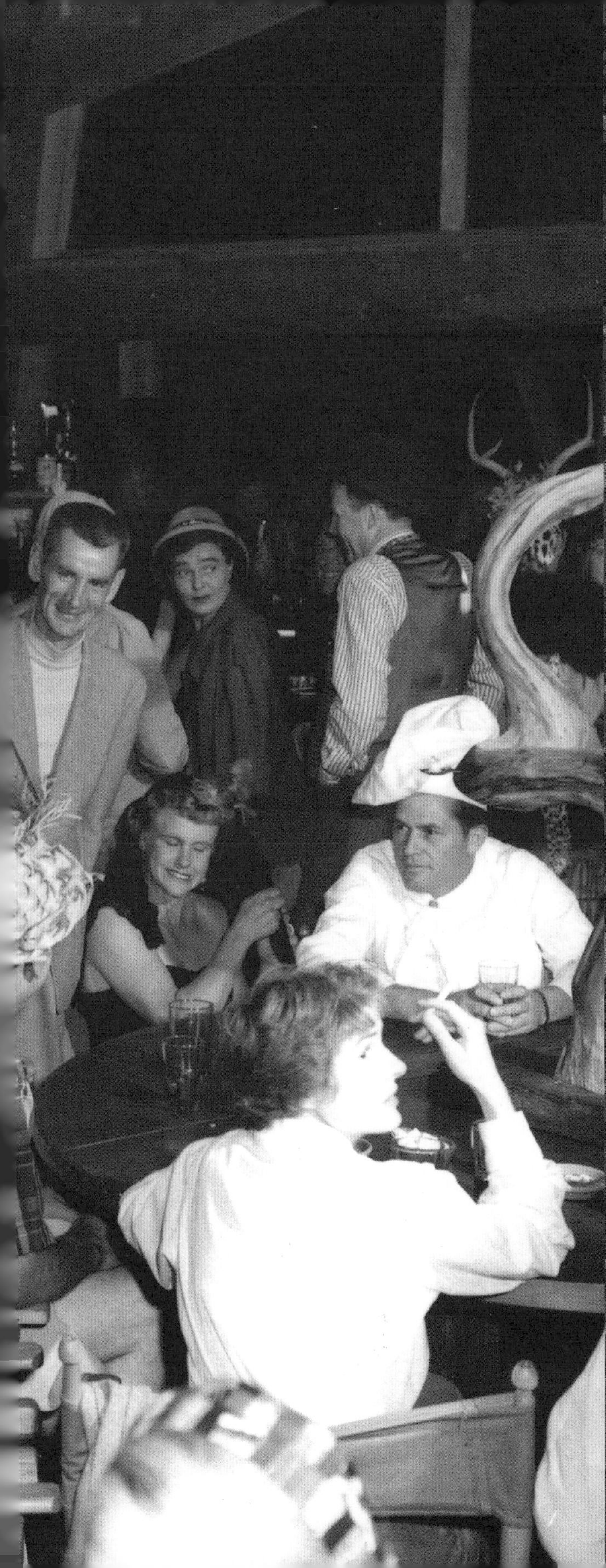

CHAPTER 3

Bohemian Nepenthe

Kaffe and Dorcas

Just remember that the Greek word nepenthes
means "no pain" and join in accordingly.

—PLAYBOY, 1960

{ 3 }

BOHEMIAN NEPENTHE

Big Sur in the 1950s and '60s was what Caryl Hill, then a waitress and onetime
girlfriend of author Henry Miller, called "the golden years" with "star customers."
For artists, writers, and other counterculture types, Nepenthe became a mecca, a
refuge for travelers and seekers, the famous and not so famous, and a way station for
those passing through, out of which grew the myth and legend of Nepenthe.

With a newly minted highway and recovering economy, and Henry's emerging
fame after the ban on his Tropic books lifted, people flocked to Big Sur and hence to
Nepenthe. Some created their own utopia there, like Henry, who valued the freedom
to go about his work and life free of government input. He used Nepenthe like his
private club, Caryl remembered, driving down in an old green Cadillac and carrying
on "intellectual discussions" with my grandfather at the bar.

The beat poets followed, and the restaurant became their favorite haunt outside
of San Francisco. Jack Kerouac came and ate "heaven burgers," drank Manhattans,
and rallied his cohorts along for the ride. Writer Richard Brautigan "honkey-tonked"
at Nepenthe for a couple of days on his way out of town. In a fit of desperation, he
once pleaded with Caryl, "You've got to take me home with you, [because] I've got
Scorpio rising."

Nepenthe became a gathering place for many distinguished artists, painters, sculptors,
writers, musicians, and architects who lived in Big Sur, an extended living room away
from home. For years the bar exuded a lively, if not literary, presence. Author and
wildman Dennis Murphy was said to have gotten into a fight with a sculptor friend

at the bar that sent Dennis to the hospital with stab wounds. "Every night was like Halloween night, almost out of control," remembered Clovis Harrod, who arrived in 1959 and worked there through the early '80s.

Employees called the far side of the bar "Dirty Corner" because it was where Henry hung out and told his bawdy tales and where the poet Eric Barker recited his dirty limericks, sometimes while standing on top of the bar. Anthropologist Giles Healey captivated guests with stories about the Mayans and other tales; when prompted, sculptor and sometime-bartender Harry Dick Ross recited lines from his wife's song, "South Coast: The Ballad of Big Sur," about a man who wins his wife in a card game, a Kingston Trio hit also made famous by American folk master Ramblin' Jack Elliot. Ruth Sawyer, known as Madam Ruth, a former madam and informal keeper of Nepenthe until she died in 1977, on one occasion danced the striptease with actress Kim Novak, who lived in the area and often hung out there.

My grandfather reveled in Nepenthe's reputation and celebrated guest list. "I was tending bar one night, and I looked up and there was Henry Miller, Man Ray, and Anaïs Nin," he used to say. On any given occasion he added people to the list, like Salvador Dalí. He loved to carry on about Henry, especially one evening when he beat him in Ping-Pong. He relayed it at my grandmother's memorial in 1986: "One night at 2:00 a.m., I heard a knock on the cabin door and it was Henry in his bathrobe. He always used to wander around in his bathrobe. He said he had a dream in which his astrologer had told him he could beat me. So I took him down-stairs, gave him a swig of Courvoisier, and then proceeded to beat the hell out of him. Lolly suggested he get a new astrologer."

> *Never let the truth get in the way of a good story.*
>
> —BILL FASSETT

Poet Dylan Thomas came in with his wife, too drunk to make conversation so he drew all over the napkins. "I should have kept those things," my grandfather lamented in an interview. "I never had a discussion with him. He just stared at me, drunk as hell." Dylan had been to a literary tea and someone told him to go to Nepenthe, the "nearest bar to Paris." Dylan looked like hell and died three months later, he added.

Actor Steve McQueen dropped in many times, once "zooming to the restaurant on his motorcycle with his wife on the back, and they only had enough money to split a hamburger," my grandfather marveled. The late William Claxton, a jazz photographer, captured a contemplative McQueen sitting in front of a blazing outdoor fire on the terrace in 1964.

My grandfather liked to say how this young, fresh-faced kid just out of the army stopped in on his way south, hoping to make it big in Hollywood. He poured him a drink, bid him good luck, and sent him on his way. That was Clint Eastwood. He starred in *Rawhide* soon after, and later bought the Carmel Mission Ranch where my grandfather rented a cabin. They occasionally played tennis at the beach club.

Lolly, Bill, and Henry Miller

Sculptor Harry Dick Ross manning the bar

Bill Fassett and friends, 1950s

Ruth Sawyer

Ruth arrived at Nepenthe in 1959, a feisty gun-moll type from Hollywood, and stayed on as my grandparents' right hand and close friend. She pulled up in a convertible one gloriously sunny afternoon, then sauntered across the terrace wearing hot pants and high heels and dragging a fur coat, with her chauffeur ten paces behind. She caught the eye of everyone there, including bartender Tom Sawyer. "Oh God, I'm in love," he said. Within a year she married him.

Ruth presided over the restaurant, sitting at one corner of the bar dressed in something gorgeous, a long cigarette dangling seductively between her fingers. Other times she sat at the middle half-round table playing dominoes with my grandfather. She ended the evenings by saying to guests, "You don't have to go home, but you can't stay here."

Sick with cancer in the last few years of her life, one morning she gathered everyone in the alcove for a final good-bye. Wearing a fur coat over her nightclothes, she announced, "I'm going to have the Champagne now." We all had a toast, even us kids. She told my grandfather that when she died, he was to "rent a damn plane to throw her ashes over Las Vegas."

COCKTAILS

Nepenthe's early menu was heavy on cocktails with whimsical names and descriptions, some revisited today in the more upbeat urban cocktail scene, but others uniquely our own. The Original Nepenthe C & C, a mixture of warmed Chartreuse and Cognac, had "bouquet, fire, and velvet," and was "richer than a box at the opera, a string of pearls, or a sable foot stool," extolled the menu. The Avante Garde Crème de Menthe Frappe was "a towering green jewel, such as you have never seen or tasted before." The bar also served Strega, an Italian saffron-laced liqueur, used to flavor the famous Torta Caprese (page 16), an almond cake from the island in Italy where my grandmother lived.

We sold imported Mumm Champagne for $12.50 a bottle and local Sonoma Pinot Noir for $2.25, or $.35 a glass. If desired, guests could order the Drink of Authority: two jiggers of 25-year-old Scotch with 16 ounces of soda for $2.00, which was also the price of a 3-quart pitcher of beer.

Meeting at the bar on Sunday afternoons was a favorite pastime, when many guests drove down from Pebble Beach to make a day of it, and old and new friends gathered to hear the latest round of stories and drink festive cocktails.

Moscow Mule

This sharp, gingery drink was served for a time in a copper metal cup with a kicking mule insignia, a marketing scheme by the creators of the drink and popularized in Hollywood. It became a Nepenthe classic. Pour 2 ounces Smirnoff vodka into a glass filled with ice, top with 4 ounces ginger beer and a squeeze of lime, and garnish with a slice of raw cucumber.

The Original Nepenthe C & C

"Let one seep through your bones."

Heat a snifter glass by steaming it over a boiling kettle for a few seconds or swirling it with hot water. Pour in ¾ ounce Courvoisier, then a scant ¾ ounce Chartreuse.

Nepenthe's Gay Pavilion

Folk dancing played a major role in the myth and legend of Nepenthe. My family taught the guests the Rye Waltz, the Cotton-Eyed Joe, and other popular dances such as the rumba, tango, and Varsuviana, and they joined in accordingly. The Fassett kids performed almost nightly. "My youngest daughter, Kim, will now dance with her older brother Kaffe," my grandfather would announce over the loudspeaker, and everyone would stop to watch.

As a teenager, Uncle Kaffe brought ethnic folk dance to the mix. He attended the arts-oriented Happy Valley School in Ojai, where he was taught Ukrainian dance as part of the curriculum. In turn, he taught everyone back at home. When the music came on, waiters, dishwashers, bartenders, and cooks danced. "Everyone would drop what they were doing," recalled my aunt Holly.

Cole Weston's first wife, Helen, worked at Nepenthe as a waitress. She wore bright red underwear beneath her long black skirts that showed when she twirled. My grandmother bought her girls red underwear, too, and once a customer complained that kids on the terrace were showing off their underclothes, not realizing it was part of the act.

Henry Miller applauded the Fassett children in *Big Sur and the Oranges of Hieronymus Bosch,* his book about living in Big Sur: "As it is, they have a wonderful roller-skating rink in the dance floor, which adjoins the dining room and bar outdoors. Evenings, before the place gets too crowded, the whole gang of them entertains the guests doing folk dances. They have a repertoire which would do credit to a professional dancer. To watch Kim, the youngest, who is still only a bit of a tot, is a delight. She floats about as if she were in heaven. They need no supervision and they get none. When they're weary they retire, to listen in quiet to a Beethoven quartet, Sibelius or an album of Shankar."

BILL OF FARE

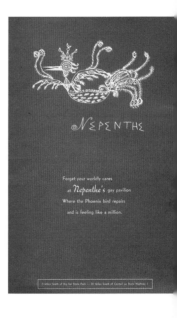

Nepenthe opened for lunch on weekends in the mid-1950s, with a ham platter, assorted sandwiches (liverwurst, deviled egg, and fried ham to name a few), and a choice of salads. On Sundays they offered brunch (starting at 11:30 a.m.) of little pig sausages and eggs, cinnamon apple rings, french fries, and individual coffee cakes with coffee, a complete smorgasbord for $1.50.

The dinner menu featured prime steaks aged on the premises for the "Carnivorous Epicure": a filet mignon or New York steak, and two ground steak dinners, including the Ambrosia Burger (page 65), spelled Ambrosiaburger, as one word. They later added roasted squab, to become Lolly's Roast Chicken (page 113), and grilled fish. For dessert, they served a cheese and cracker plate (a wedge of imported Camembert or blue cheese accompanied by a crisp apple, olives, sliced carrots and pickles, and a basket of crackers), or a slice of cake and a pot of tea, "not in the bag," but "of the essence," an important distinction still maintained today.

In the beginning my grandfather halted service while the staff ate. At the end of the week, he occasionally served them steak ends, saved as a treat. On employee birthdays, they served cake and Champagne, and this is how the astrology parties began. Sign parties, based on the monthly astrological signs, were staged monthly and grew to be so large that they had to be ended in the early 2000s. People drove from as far as San Francisco and Los Angeles to revel in the free Champagne and cake and dance until midnight on the terrace, under the stars.

*O*ut of the feeling that the site and its magnificent vistas was too vast, too wonderful to keep to themselves—"no individual can own it, it belongs to everyone," said Lolly—grew the idea of NEPENTHE, an isle of no-care. It developed through a building, so conceived and executed as to belong to no time and to all time. In it were used native materials—redwood and adobe—and so used that the building became one with the landscape and the earth it stands on.

The PHOENIX was chosen as the standard of our NEPENTHE, because of its particular significance. According to legend, the bird, with wings of gold and jewelled plumage, returned from Arabia to the temple of Heliopolis every five hundred years, to burn itself on the altar and arise from its own ashes, more magnificent than ever— a symbol of immortality.

—FROM THE BACK OF THE NEPENTHE MENU

3 green onions, finely chopped
2 teaspoons granulated sugar
1 clove garlic, finely chopped,
   or ¾ teaspoon granulated garlic
1 heaping tablespoon dried oregano,
   or 2 to 3 tablespoons fresh
1 heaping tablespoon dried tarragon,
   or 2 to 3 tablespoons fresh
1 teaspoon salt
1¼ teaspoons coarsely ground black pepper
1 (12-ounce) can garbanzo beans (about 2 cups),
   drained and rinsed
1 (12-ounce) can kidney beans (about 2 cups),
   drained and rinsed
½ cup olive oil or good-quality vegetable oil
2 or 3 tablespoons red wine vinegar

Garbanzo and Kidney Bean Salad

At the restaurant, we call the process of making this salad the "six and six," meaning six No. 10 cans of each type of beans per batch. The beans are drained, then rinsed and layered in a clean tub with herbs, added in by the handful. Oil and vinegar fill the tub to the brim. It sits overnight before it's stirred and packed into boat-shaped bowls with a slotted spoon.

Dotty Lopes created this house favorite in the '50s, one of three sides offered with a sandwich. It was also served as a three-way menu item with two other lunch salads, and black bread in a basket. To replicate the layering technique, make it in an upright 2-quart plastic container with a lid. After layering the herbs and beans, cover with oil and add ¼ to ½ cup vinegar, then fill with more oil. Leave undisturbed overnight in the refrigerator. Toss well, and serve.

Combine the onions, sugar, garlic, oregano, tarragon, salt, and pepper in a large bowl. Add the garbanzo beans, kidney beans, oil, and vinegar and toss. Cover and refrigerate for at least an hour. The salad is best if it is made a day ahead, allowing the flavors to meld. Adjust seasoning as necessary before serving.

Serve chilled as a side to picnic fare, sandwiches, or on a bed of crisped lettuce, as it is done at the restaurant.

1 (10- to 14-pound) partially or fully cooked smoked
  bone-in ham, or a smaller boneless ham
¾ cup firmly packed brown sugar
⅓ cup brown mustard
¼ teaspoon ground cloves
Whole cloves

Dotty's Baked Ham with Mustard-Brown Sugar Glaze

The sweet, spicy scent of baking ham with cloves wafting from the oven takes me right back home and to the daily grind at Nepenthe: coating the hams with the thick sugar glaze; seasoning the beef to roast for sandwiches; making the bean salad, the coleslaw dressing, ambrosia sauce, and the cheese pies. This was the daily work of the prep cook, a job I helped with as a young person. We loved to sneak a trim of ham just after we pulled it from the oven, the salty-sweet taste lingering on our tongue making us want more and more.

This recipe came from Dotty Lopes, who started the lunches at Nepenthe in the '50s. Her daughter Willie told me that she used to pour 7UP over it to seal the glaze and make it that much sweeter and candylike.

Preheat the oven to 350°F.

Remove the rind (skin) from the ham unless the butcher has done this for you. Trim any excess fat, leaving a thin layer. Score the fat side, about ¼-inch-thick, in a diamond pattern. Place the ham in a shallow roasting pan fat side up. Make a paste with the brown sugar, mustard, and ground cloves and rub it onto the ham, covering the scored side completely. Press a clove into each shape, or at each diamond point.

Add a glassful of water to the pan and loosely cover with aluminum foil. Bake for 15 to 18 minutes per pound, basting as desired, or until the internal temperature reaches desired temperature (no less than 140°F). Remove the foil 30 minutes before done. Let cool 15 minutes before transferring to a platter. Reserve the bone and any trimmings for soup stock.

SERVES 6 TO 8

DRESSING
½ cup Best Foods mayonnaise
1½ teaspoons granulated sugar
1½ teaspoons brown sugar
¾ teaspoon granulated garlic
Chinese hot mustard
¾ teaspoon salt
Scant pinch white pepper
3 tablespoons red wine vinegar

SLAW
1 medium cabbage
Paprika
Black olives, for garnish

Crunchy Coleslaw

To maintain its crunch and texture, coleslaw should be made with fresh green cabbage, not preshredded from a bag, and not drenched so that it becomes soggy quickly. I like it clean, crisp, and only faintly sweet with a touch of sour; not mixed with carrots, peanuts, onions, apple, or purple cabbage; only lightly coated with dressing; and dusted with a little bit of smoky paprika at the end.

This recipe calls for Best Foods mayonnaise (called Hellmann's in the East) and Chinese hot mustard. The coleslaw just doesn't taste the same without them. It makes 1 cup dressing, enough to coat about 8 cups freshly cut slaw, or 1 medium cabbage. You can make the dressing ahead, store it in the refrigerator up to a week, and dress only as much salad as you plan to eat in one sitting.

For the dressing, mix the mayonnaise, granulated sugar, brown sugar, granulated garlic, a scant ¼ teaspoon mustard (or more or less to taste), salt, and pepper in a medium bowl, stirring until smooth. Gradually whisk in the vinegar, stopping after 2 tablespoons to taste, as some vinegars are stronger than others. Add the remaining vinegar or 1 tablespoon water to thin.

For the salad, peel away and discard the outer leaves of the cabbage. Thinly slice the remaining cabbage with a heavy, sharp knife. In a large bowl, toss a desired amount of the dressing with the cabbage, using your hands to thoroughly coat. Serve in individual bowls, each dusted with paprika and garnished with a black olive.

MAKES 1 COFFEE CAKE, SERVING 8 TO 12

TOPPING
½ cup firmly packed brown sugar
1 cup chopped walnuts
2 teaspoons cinnamon
1 green apple, peeled and cored

CAKE
1 cup (2 sticks) butter
¾ cup granulated sugar
3 eggs
1 cup sour cream
1 teaspoon pure vanilla extract
3 cups flour
2 teaspoons baking powder
1 teaspoon baking soda
Dash nutmeg
Pinch salt

Sour Cream–Apple Coffee Cake

This cake, based on a recipe from our family kitchen archives, is an old-fashioned, moist coffee cake with chopped apples. Perfect for that late-morning cup of coffee or as part of a smorgasbord breakfast such as Nepenthe presented in the mid-1950s.

Preheat the oven to 350°F. Lightly butter and flour a small tube or Bundt pan, knocking out excess flour.

For the topping, mix the brown sugar, walnuts, and cinnamon in a bowl. Chop the apples into small bite-size pieces and set aside (toss with a little lemon if they begin to discolor quickly).

For the cake, using an electric mixer, beat the butter with the granulated sugar in a large bowl until light and fluffy. Add the eggs one at a time, mixing well and scraping down the side after each addition to incorporate. Beat in the sour cream and vanilla. In a separate bowl, combine the flour, baking powder, baking soda, nutmeg, and salt. Add to the batter in three parts, mixing well after each. The batter will be quite thick.

Spread half the batter into the prepared baking pan. Sprinkle with half the apples and half the sugar mixture. Spread with the remaining batter and top with the remaining apples and sugar mixture. Bake for 1 hour, or until a toothpick inserted in the center comes out clean.

Halloween Bal Masque

Aalloween costume parties started as a way to mark the end of Nepenthe's work season, when the restaurant closed for the winter to reopen on April 1. An early ad for one of the parties, posted around town, shows a naked woman lying across the bar with her head back, downing a second drink, a cherry in the other hand and a stunned bartender. The bar opened at 9:00 p.m. with no food, but staff served coffee and doughnuts on the house at midnight.

Bill Worth and Kim Novak

At its start, friends and event-goers flocked to the festivities. Vying for the Best Costume award, or some other prized title like Sexiest Couple, people arrived wearing the most outrageous ensembles. My grandmother always had a closet full of costumes if someone showed up without one, including a general's jacket with brass buttons that has shown up in almost every homegrown theatre production over the years, as did all the flamenco costumes and petticoats. Eve Miller, wife of Henry, once arrived in an extravagant butterfly costume with fanciful wings. Henry's third wife, Lepska, is also pictured to the right having her fortune read. One year a couple all the way from La Jolla wore only fig leaves and won top prize. Amelia Newell, former wife of sculptor Gordon Newell, one year showed up as a shower, wearing only cellophane and Stilettos. She was the talk of the town for years.

There were other stories, like the couple that came impromptu, wearing only their birthday suits. Artist Edmund Kara often outdid himself, one year arriving as a bird, dressed head to toe in carefully shredded newspaper and wearing black round glasses. In the late '70s, employee Clovis Harrod came as a Nepenthe Chef Salad, and builder Walter Trotter ran about dipping into her bowl, tossing out the ingredients, and asking "Do you want tossed salad?" A popular theme was to come as each other, and it was always surprising when a person was actually taken for the person they impersonated. Erica Weston and then-waitress Julie Miller came as "dirty" old men one year, and "dirty" old women the next.

Over the years, news of the annual costume event flamed, encouraging more and new guests each year. In the '80s, my aunt Holly had the idea to turn the party into a fund-raiser with all the Ambrosia Burgers that guests could eat. Today it continues in the tradition of yesterday's theatrics, slightly tamer but still very much celebrated, and is a benefit for the Big Sur Volunteer Fire Brigade.

COUNTERCULTURE IN THE 1960s

In the 1960s, with its known counterculture and wild beauty, Big Sur provided an oasis for people looking to get away from it all. At Nepenthe guests could spend a dollar and stay a day, or if they were hungry and without, wash dishes in exchange for a meal. Some people stayed for days, months, and even years. My grandmother likened Nepenthe to one big open living room. "It had a destiny for people to come and go," she said, concluding that Big Sur "chooses its own, in a kind of way."

The 1960s brought change and a cultural shift to Nepenthe, as was similarly reflected across the nation. The children were growing up. Griff, the oldest son, married in 1960, and both he and Kaffe had moved away, for good, by 1965. By this time, the first of many grandchildren had arrived, including my cousin Kirk, his sister Erin, my brother, Cap, and myself, born in 1965. Our mothers were young, our fathers were gone, and our grandparents cared for us most of the time, especially our grand-mother, who watched over us routinely. We called them Mom and Dad (or Daddy Bill) and often refer to them that way still.

Kirk and Lolly

By the late '60s, my grandfather, perhaps yearning for something more, spent time away from the property, traveling to Asia with the Pebble Beach Club and to Europe for pleasure. Eventually, he began keeping a room at the Carmel Mission Ranch and developed a whole other life outside of Nepenthe. Through it all, my grandmother stayed at the restaurant. Once, following a forceful encounter with my grandfather, who was worried about their financial situation, she affirmed her own feelings about what they had created. "I have been sitting on this hill all this time trying to preserve as far as possible, the essence of Nepenthe."

When we were little, we all slept on my grandmother's big bed in her back room, a memory impressed into my skin like the smell of the witch hazel that she dabbed on my forehead when I couldn't sleep.

She read us the Lord's Prayer, and tucked the sheets tightly around us so we couldn't get out of bed, remembered my cousin Erin.

Holly, wearing Bill Gibb design

Big Sur and Popular Culture

The vigor of the '60s brought a surge of interest in the coastal hamlet of Big Sur. Hearst Castle in Cambria opened in 1959, bringing tourists from the south, and in 1962, the Esalen Institute opened its doors to the Human Potential Movement, drawing its own illustrious crowd. The folk music scene and hippies followed, as did the arrival of New Age groups in the late '60s, among them the Maharishi Mahesh Yogi, founder of Transcendental Meditation, who was once ceremoniously carried across the terrace on a flower-adorned platform. He later wrote a spiritual "Menu for Nepenthe" and presented it to Mary Belle Sheld (now Snow), the manager at the time, who kept it in the safe for years.

After a brief attempt to open a sandwich shop in Monterey in 1959, "a miniature Lindy's," as my grandfather once crowed, my grandparents reenergized their commitment to their growing enterprise. (They named the shop Symposium, meaning a "merry feast," according to my grandfather's dictionary. "Food for Gods and Mortals too" was its tagline, though it closed within its first year.) By 1963, they began work on a new addition, the Phoenix Shop, a treasure trove of worldly goods, on the south-facing ledge below the restaurant. The Shop started out of my grandmother's love for junk shopping and collecting unusual items from around the world. She had a tremendous eye for fashion and style, as was evident by the colorful tailored smocks, influenced by Asian patterns and design, that she had made for herself. She later partnered with a friend who collected Chinese antiques, and they sold them at the shop and out of his Victorian home in Pacific Grove.

Early on, Caryl Hill and my grandmother frequented tag sales and made trips to San Francisco, mining the streets of Chinatown for "cast-offs" and bringing them back to sell. Caryl brought a "shabby blue" corner cabinet from a house she lived at above Deetjens that they would "wheel down on to the terrace." They called it the Gazebo, and from it they sold items they collected. Later my grandmother stationed a wood and glass gazebo on the Phoenix roof, and it became the first clothing boutique.

Following the 1963 Monterey Folk Festival, folk concerts at Esalen, and "Celebration at Big Sur" (one of seven concerts convened by Joan Baez and the title of a documentary film on the same subject, in which my brother and myself are shown dancing on the deck), a coterie of music followers and friends ended up at Nepenthe. "We who worked at Nepenthe in the '60s were very full of ourselves," remembered Tenny Chonin, who also worked for Judy Collins at the time. Describing their attitude as aloof but not rude, she said when tourists asked the meaning of the name "Nepenthe," the waitstaff told them it was "Greek for expensive." It didn't seem to stop them from coming, perpetually lured by the bohemian mystique that permeated the place. "My best memories are the nights after closing," she remembered, "when we'd all go out to the terrace and dance, Santa Anas blowing warm winds across the terrace, and the moon was full and bright and you could clearly see the mountains."

Rita Gatti, a young folk singer, arrived at Nepenthe soon after meeting Joan Baez at the Monterey Folk Festival. The festival is where she "discovered Big Sur" as she put it, inaugurating ten years of living there. Rita performed at several Esalen concerts with the Big Sur Choir (see photo, page 117) and became "local color" at Eduardo Tirella's celebrity-filled parties. (Eduardo, an interior designer who lived across from Nepenthe, was close friends with Kim Novak, who frequented the restaurant. Besides working on *The Sandpiper* film, he designed gardens for tobacco heiress Doris Duke, who inadvertently killed him in a car accident at her home.) Rita began working at Nepenthe midwinter, during one of its annual closures, and worked her way up from dishwasher to chef, and later became the family cook. She remembered the after-hours scene at Nepenthe fondly. "The nights after closing the grill were memorable. By then we were crazy tired, maybe slightly buzzed. Shively would give me vodka tonics and I gave him steak sandwiches all night long. Dancing was the greatest way to unwind and socialize and it sometimes went on way late, until the neighbors called and complained."

Adding to the festivities, Nepenthe's staff became known for their unique dress in a riot of color. My grandmother encouraged the staff to wear festive clothing. Early on, the young women wore long tiered skirts in colorful layers or wide-legged pants with Capri sandals and espadrilles. She wanted them to look timeless. A bartender in the '60s wore purple jeans, knee-high leather moccasins, and fringed vests. Waiters were said to be barefoot and carefree, without watches or attention to time. Others wore ethnic caftans or knitted vests, and one hostess who on occasion wore a "strapless, cut to mid thigh blue sequined gown," said waitress Sylvia Rudolph, who worked at Nepenthe for thirty-five years, and made her own long skirts, one a patchwork of worn blue jeans.

Alice Russell, who managed the Phoenix Shop for close to ten years starting in the late 1960s, arrived on the scene from England to be with my grandfather. She had owned a clothing boutique in London with the designer Bill Gibb and had met my grandfather on one of his trips to visit Kaffe. He encouraged her to come out to work for him (without telling her of his family situation, nor advising my grandmother of his plan), which she did, initially causing great distress between my grandparents. (She and Lolly eventually made amends, working closely together in the later years; in 1974 Alice and my grandfather had a beautiful daughter, Havrah.) As manager of the Phoenix Shop, she brought in popular clothing designers and unusual gift items from Europe, and staged weekly fashion shows on the terrace. Alice also brought over an Italian seamstress, who worked out of the sewing room to create one-off designs for the shop. Geangy, the eccentric fortune-teller, artist, and friend to my grandmother, created her own, offbeat line of clothing for the shop as well.

It was Alice who taught my uncle Kaffe how to knit, on a train ride home from a Scottish wool mill, where he bought twenty colors of Shetland wool, thus helping start his career as a knitware designer. *Vogue Knitting* featured his first design. Kaffe eventually became the first living textile artist to have a one-man show at the Victoria and Albert Museum in London, where he has lived and worked since 1965.

Fashion Shows

Nepenthe presented fashion shows on the terrace starting in the '50s, with waiters and waitresses as models. "Creations by Sabater," by designer and dancer John Sabater, who had an atelier in Big Sur, was one of the early presentations. It included an edict by Henry Miller, who described fashion as meaningless unless it catered to the individual person. "Just as each one thinks, walks, talks in his own unique way, so one should dress," he ranted, and further suggested women avoid the "sacks of oatmeal" proffered by mainstream fashion designers.

My uncle Kaffe and London designer Bill Gibb collaborated on designs that were first debuted at Nepenthe in 1971, a "fashion fairy-tale" extravaganza according to the paper. Fashion shows occured throughout the 1970s.

Phoenix Shop

Opened in 1964 and designed by architects Hall and Goodhue of Monterey, the Phoenix Shop was dubbed a "Turkish Bazaar" by the press. The Phoenix Shop highlighted handcrafted items from Big Sur artists, antique jewelry, and handmade clothing and knitwear created by my grandmother and others who sewed for her in the "sewing room," where she housed bolts of fabrics and several sewing machines. The Phoenix was one of the first to carry a selection of American Indian jewelry, very prized at the time, bought directly from reservations in New Mexico and Arizona.

Caryl operated her Ananga Ranga Trading Co. out of the shop, offering a $400 tiger skin said to "generate electricity" and having something to do with the Hindu Vedas and its sixty-four positions for making love. Over the years the Phoenix became known for its one-of-a-kind designs and continues to sell original knitwear by my uncle, Kaffe Fassett, and handcrafts by other family members.

The bottom floor of the Phoenix, now a boutique, initially opened as a café serving coffee and sandwiches during the winter months when the restaurant was closed. It later morphed into a stained-glass studio and at one time housed a flock of pigeons in the dovecote at the far back corner of the boutique. The shop's gourmet department sold beer, wine, and cheeses for picnickers, encouraging people to come down for the day, suggesting anything they needed could be purchased on site.

At the Phoenix Shop one day in the early '60s, actress Shelley Winters pointed to a dress worn by salesperson Ronni Sloan (DeCarlo) and declared, "That's it. That's the dress I've been looking for!" It was an empire style dress of Ronni's own design made from blue and white madras fabric. When she replied that she couldn't possibly make another one since she really didn't know how to sew and that this one was a fluke, Winters told her, "Don't be ridiculous. If you did it once, you can do it again." She then handed Ronni a check for $150 and told her to deliver it posthaste to the Anaheim Theatre, where she was starring in Tennessee Williams's Sweet Bird of Youth. *And three weeks later Ronni did.*

SERVES 4

SOUR CREAM–CAPER SAUCE
⅓ cup sour cream
1 tablespoon minced onion
1 tablespoon capers, chopped
½ teaspoon hot mustard
Scant ½ teaspoon horseradish
2 tablespoons fresh lemon juice
Dash Tabasco sauce
Pinch salt and a pinch white pepper
1 tablespoon finely chopped fresh parsley or dill

FISH
2 (12-ounce) swordfish steaks, about ½ inch thick,
    halved to make 4 pieces
2 or 3 tablespoons olive oil
Sea salt and freshly ground black pepper
Lemon halves and wedges

Grilled Swordfish with Sour Cream–Caper Sauce

Nepenthe first served grilled swordfish in the '50s or '60s as a special, and my grandmother topped it with a savory sour cream–caper sauce. We used to brush the swordfish with butter while grilling, but I prefer to drizzle with olive oil beforehand as they do in Italy, where I imagine my grandmother first enjoyed this meaty Mediterranean fish. Serve the steaks on beds of young greens, either arugula or baby spinach, so that the greens wilt from the heat.

For the sauce, mix the sour cream, onion, capers, mustard, and horseradish in a small bowl. Stir in the lemon juice, Tabasco, salt, and pepper. Stir in the parsley. The sauce can be made 1 day ahead; cover and refrigerate. Bring to room temperature before serving.

For the fish, heat a grill or a grill pan over medium-high heat. Drizzle the steaks with olive oil, season with salt and pepper, and set aside for 10 minutes.

Grill the swordfish, turning only once, for 7 to 8 minutes per side for medium-rare. Just before it is done, squeeze the lemon halves over the fish. Arrange the steak on plates and drizzle with the caper sauce, or serve the sauce on the side. Serve with lemon wedges.

SERVES 4 TO 6

4 to 6 fresh sardines, cleaned and filleted
1 clove garlic, thinly sliced
3 or 4 slices lemon and/or orange
1 sprig fresh thyme
2 tablespoons chopped fresh parsley or mint
¼ cup olive oil
Freshly ground black pepper
1 tablespoon good-quality red wine vinegar, or juice of 1 lemon

Marinated Fresh Monterey Sardines

When I was growing up, Nepenthe served sardine sandwiches made with imported canned sardines, a luxury item then, on thin slices of black bread with mayonnaise and leafy, green lettuce, along with a wedge of lemon and a thick slice of purple onion. I remember sneaking the sardine tins from the dry storage, peeling back the shiny lids with a church key, and then fingering out the oily fish, eating the delicate fillets with saltine crackers. Nepenthe's sardine sandwich had a cult following but drifted off the menu in the early '70s.

Monterey was once known for its canned sardine industry and the health of its fishery, before it went under in the late 1950s. Today, Pacific sardine stocks are flourishing again, and the small, oily fish are making a comeback on the culinary scene. I like to purchase fresh whole sardines and marinate them with a touch of citrus and garlic, like ceviche. Layer slices on toasted baguette or German-style bread with a little Garlic Basil Aioli (page 276) or mayonnaise, then top with a few leaves of arugula or mâche and a thin slice of lemon for a dressed-up version of how we served it at Nepenthe long ago.

Place the sardines in a nonreactive shallow dish with the garlic and lemon slices. Stem the thyme and scatter over the fish with the parsley. Cover with the oil. Grind some fresh pepper over the top and drizzle with the vinegar. Cover tightly with plastic wrap and refrigerate for at least 2 hours or up to 1 day, occasionally turning the sardines over so that they marinate evenly.

SERVES 4 TO 6

STUFFING
3 tablespoons butter
1½ large onions, chopped
4 ribs celery, chopped
2 tablespoons chopped fresh sage, or 2 teaspoons dried
4 or 5 cups croutons, preferably sourdough
¼ to ½ cup chicken broth (optional)
Salt and freshly ground black pepper

CHICKEN
1 (4- to 5-pound) roasting chicken, split in half
2 or 3 tablespoons butter, softened
Salt and freshly ground black pepper
Paprika
Chopped fresh sage

Lolly's Roast Chicken with Sage Stuffing

This is my grandmother's recipe and a long-standing house favorite for dinner. Each guest receives half of a roasted chicken served on a bed of moist sage stuffing with Cranberry Sauce (page 114). On Thanksgiving and Christmas it is served throughout the day.

I have adapted the recipe to serve a family at home using 1 whole chicken, split in half. Ask your butcher to do this for you, or halve it yourself, cutting out the backbone and reserving it for stock. Or use a whole chicken with the same ingredients, roasting for 1¼ hours or until the thigh juices run clear when pricked with a fork.

For the stuffing, I make my own croutons using day-old artisan bread (you can toast them lightly in the oven to help dry them out), and use fresh herbs rather than dried with a little chicken broth added for moisture. If roasting a whole chicken, bake the stuffing separately, covered, for about 50 minutes.

For the stuffing, heat the butter in a large, heavy skillet over medium-high heat. Add the onions, celery, and sage and sauté until very soft. Add half the croutons, stir well, and then add the remaining croutons. Remove from the heat. Stir in broth if the stuffing seems dry. Season with salt and pepper. Cover and let sit for 10 minutes. Stir again to distribute moisture evenly and cover. When ready to use, transfer the stuffing to a baking dish or large cast-iron skillet that holds both chicken halves.

Preheat the oven to 450°F.

Rinse the bird halves and pat dry. Rub the softened butter all over the chicken and under its skin. Season all over with salt and pepper. Place the chicken on top of the stuffing. Sprinkle with the paprika and a little more chopped sage.

Roast for 15 minutes, then reduce heat to 375°F. Continue roasting for about 45 minutes or longer (depending on the size of the chicken), until golden brown and the juices run clear when you prick the meatier part of the thigh. Cover with foil if the chicken is browning too quickly.

When ready, serve directly from the pan set on a hot plate at the center of the table, or transfer the chicken to a cutting board and cut into pieces, then place on a platter with the stuffing. If roasting a whole bird, allow it to rest 10 to 15 minutes before carving.

MAKES ABOUT 1½ CUPS, SERVING 6 TO 8

3 cups (12 ounces) fresh or frozen cranberries
¾ cup granulated sugar
Zest and juice (about ⅓ cup) of 1 orange
½ cinnamon stick

Cranberry Sauce

Serve this tasty cranberry sauce with Lolly's Roast Chicken with Sage Stuffing (page 113), as we do at the restaurant at Christmas. This recipe makes enough for several dinners and also freezes well in small batches for longer storage.

Combine the cranberries, sugar, orange zest, juice, and cinnamon in a medium saucepan. Bring to a boil, and then decrease heat to low. Simmer, stirring occasionally, for 10 to 15 minutes, until the cranberries pop and the sauce thickens. It will thicken more as it cools. Store in the refrigerator.

CRUST
7 sheets graham crackers
¼ cup (½ stick) butter, melted

FILLING
1½ cups (12 ounces) cream cheese, room temperature
6 tablespoons granulated sugar
2 eggs
1 teaspoon pure vanilla extract

TOPPING
1 cup sour cream
1½ tablespoons granulated sugar
1 teaspoon pure vanilla extract

Nepenthe Cheese Pie

Our cheese pie is light and creamy and not dense like a cheesecake. My aunt Holly always says there are three ways to mess it up: first by overcooking the crust, second by overcooking the filling, and third by overcooking the topping, so "do not leave kitchen while baking these sensitive little things," as it instructs on the original recipe. Some people like to adorn it with berries or add a fruit sauce when serving, but I think it is best just as it is.

Preheat the oven to 350°F.

To make the crust, crush the crackers into fine crumbs using a rolling pin. Place in a bowl and stir in the melted butter. Ease into a 9-inch pie pan and gently press evenly onto the bottom and side, making sure the crumbs don't pile up in the middle. Bake for 5 minutes.

To make the filling, using an electric mixer, mix the cream cheese, sugar, eggs, and vanilla until smooth. Pour into the baked pie shell. Bake for 15 to 20 minutes, until set but still slightly jiggly in the middle. Cool on a rack for 15 minutes. Decrease the oven temperature to 325°F.

Make the topping. Combine the sour cream, sugar, and vanilla in a bowl.

When the pie is cool, gently spread the topping over the pie (use an offset spatula if you have one). Be careful not to upset the filling. Bake for 5 to 7 minutes, until the topping is just set, but not brown. Cool on a rack. Chill before serving.

THE CELEBRITY SCENE

In 1964 MGM filmed scenes of *The Sandpiper* on the Nepenthe terrace, starring Elizabeth Taylor, Richard Burton, and Eva Marie Saint. Taylor dined with Burton at Nepenthe daily during filming. *The Sandpiper* producer Martin Ransohoff celebrated Nepenthe's folk dance scene in the movie, bringing Nepenthe a great deal of attention. Marty had a house in Big Sur and became friends with my grandparents through their mutual friends Edmund Kara and Eduardo Tirella, both of whom contributed to the film.

Television spots were filmed at Nepenthe as well. Dionne Warwick and Mac Davis both performed on the terrace, as did Percy Sledge, who sang "When a Man Loves a Woman" with a row of go-go dancers dancing on the long, bench-like table behind him, the painterly view as backdrop.

Nepenthe stayed a magnet for the Hollywood set, musicians, and artists throughout the 1960s and early 1970s. The cast and crew from Robert Dillon's *The French Connection* dropped by during filming on the coast. Jimi Hendrix, Janis Joplin, and Mama Cass Elliot hung around during the Monterey Pop Festival. At the boutique, Hendrix bought cool velvet vests from Afghanistan, and Mama Cass fell in love with my grandmother's hand-sewn caftans with hanging tassels. David Crosby from Crosby, Stills, and Nash had lunch at the restaurant the month after Woodstock; all the waitresses went mad for him. Harlem Renaissance poet Langston Hughes stopped there once and read his poems, as did the Oxford poet Stephen Spender. Musician Ravi Shankar dined there with his family, and hipster performer Lord Buckley hung out there in 1960, the same year he died.

Management had a general policy to leave these people alone, though not always with success. My grandmother forbid my grandfather to go to the bar the day Bing Crosby showed up. Actress Shelley Winters once danced throughout an afternoon with a handsome, younger boyfriend. She didn't have a care in the world, thanks to my grandmother.

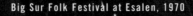

Big Sur Folk Festival at Esalen, 1970

The Sandpiper

In the spring of 2008, I interviewed Marty Ransohoff, cofounder of Filmways in the early 1950s and one of the writers and producer of the 1965 film *The Sandpiper*, in his Los Angeles home, where he recalled making the romantic drama, his fondness for Elizabeth Taylor, and why he included Nepenthe in the script.

The Sandpiper was set in Big Sur and starred Richard Burton, Elizabeth Taylor, and Eva Marie Saint. The film portrays a spirited single mother, Laura Reynolds, played by Taylor, who lives with her young son in a rustic cliffside dwelling decorated with driftwood and found objects. They spend their days combing the beach for treasures, painting, and reading Chaucer. When the son gets in trouble with the law for shooting a deer, he is ordered to attend an Episcopal boarding school where Burton is the stalwart headmaster, Dr. Edward Hewitt. He is initially appalled by Reynolds's eccentric ways, but soon finds himself taken with her after visiting her cabin. When he arrives she is tending to a wounded sandpiper, and another time posing nude for a sculptor friend, played by Charles Bronson. The small coastal bird becomes a symbol for freedom in the film.

The colorful and bizarre gaiety of a Bohemian winery is shown to conservative Richard Burton by Elizabeth Taylor

Metro-Goldwyn-Mayer and Filmways present "THE SANDPIPER" in Panavision and Metrocolor

Awash in the dramatic scenery and the lure of bohemian life, they soon begin an illicit affair (Dr. Huett is married to Claire, played by Academy Award winner Eva Marie Saint) only to end it later, discontented but marked by the experience.

The actress Kim Novak had introduced Marty to Big Sur, and he fell in love with the landscape. He bought property and built a house overlooking the ocean, where he spent time over a period spanning fifteen years. He became close friends with two artists, Edmund Kara and Eduardo Tirella, who lived across from Nepenthe, and soon befriended my grandparents.

Nepenthe had a minor role in the film, playing itself. In one scene, Reynolds (Taylor) leaves a note in her mailbox saying that she is off to Nepenthe, if anyone cares to join her. Later, when Dr. Huett (Burton) walks onto the terrace to look for her, she is sitting with a group of artist friends at a half-round table. They welcome him to the Club Nepenthe, described as nirvana in the film, and a vanishing of all things sad.

Nepenthe offered an authentic backdrop for '60s bohemian life in Big Sur. "It was part of the tapestry, part of the scene," said Marty.

Inspired by Big Sur, Marty wrote an outline of the story over a long weekend, and then offered the lead role in the film to Elizabeth Taylor. "She liked the idea of playing an artist, a free spirit," he said.

Big Sur was a haven for free spirits, and Taylor's character was very much in tune with the area: determined if not a little wild. Marty had recently built his house and "was in love with the scenery, the redwoods, the ocean," he recalled. Marlon Brando had just completed *One-Eyed Jacks* in Big Sur, and the setting seemed ripe for this kind of tale. "It was a real love story and fit nicely into Big Sur at that time," said Marty.

The film presents a conflict between what was considered conventional and what was changing in society, wherein two people from different worlds collide. That was the real spine of the story. On one hand there was this rigid, conservative set of values and on the other all this freedom and beauty

The Sandpiper had tremendous star power and won an Academy Award for its theme song, "The Shadow of Your Smile." Not bad for a thirty-eight-page outline written over a weekend by Marty, with a final draft of the screenplay written by Dalton Trumbo and Michael Wilson. The film boasted Oscar-winner Vincente Minelli as director. Taylor and Burton, married less than a year and fresh off of *Cleopatra* and *The Yellow Rolls-Royce*, were a hot item around town and a huge draw.

My grandfather loved to tell the story of how Minelli ran around the set instructing the extras to "stop looking" at the beautiful couple—to no avail. People were smitten with them. "They received a lot of attention wherever they went," Marty said. "I took them to Nepenthe and they stopped traffic."

Some of the artists and people working at the restaurant played parts as extras. My uncle Kaffe choreographed the dance

Marty and Edmund

Edmund Kara and Eduardo Errella

Edmund, a former Hollywood costume designer who made dresses for Peggy Lee and Lena Horne among others, sculpted a redwood bust of Elizabeth Taylor for *The Sandpiper*. A few years earlier, he carved the fantastic, mythical phoenix bird from a massive redwood burl that now reigns on the restaurant terrace. Rising from the ashes, it replaced the old oak tree seen in *The Sandpiper* trailer in 1976.

Like many of my grandmother's creative friends, Eduardo infused Nepenthe with his magic, contributing fantastic costumes for the annual Halloween Bal Masque, and later suggesting that Marty include the Nepenthe scene in *The Sandpiper*. Eduardo is credited as the coordinator for the Big Sur scenes in the film.

sequences for the restaurant scene and later followed the cast to Paris, where interior scenes were shot. When the film crew first came to the restaurant, my grandparents sent the kids to folk dance, something Nepenthe was known for at the time. They were later filmed for the trailer, in what San Francisco columnist Herb Caen described as "a way to explain Big Sur to the world."

MGM reserved all the tables in the restaurant in the first days of shooting, and they hired extra police and highway patrol to control the crowds. Taylor and Burton dined daily at Nepenthe after that. The crew filmed only the exterior of Nepenthe and the first scene leading up to the restaurant's terrace, never venturing inside, according to the few who remember. Most of the action centered near Soberanes Point, halfway to Carmel, where they built a beach shack, a shell of a house on the ledge of a cliff. Someone later bought the cabin and relocated it to Inverness, California.

In Paris, they shot at the Boulogne film studio, where they created an exact replica of Nepenthe, and spent days combing Left Bank bistros for bohemian types, according to a 1964 article. Some extras were brought in from Los Angeles, and at least one resident from Big Sur had a minor role.

My uncle Kaffe recalled walking onto the Paris set of Nepenthe and being amazed by how much it looked like the real thing. "It was just spooky," he said. "The details were incredible, down to the brick fireplace, chessboard, and painted coastline." He said when Taylor made her first appearance, Minelli told her to go back and come in again, because "everyone on set turned to look at her." She was too much of a towering figure to speak to, he recalled, but stunning. When one woman complained about her costume being too rough, the designer told her pointedly, "I'm designing this. It's a very bohemian joint." Initially, there were few histrionics, then someone piped up, "That's because there is one boss on this set, and that's Elizabeth Taylor."

And so *The Sandpiper* has a place in our family history. The filmmakers and crew became a part of the milieu and myth. Taylor is remembered as a real beauty with the most striking violet eyes. She once kissed my cousin Erin, then a little baby, on the cheek, stopping to do so in the middle of her dance lesson. My cousin Kirk is seen sitting on his mother's lap in the film's trailer and dawdling around the terrace in his calf-high white plastic boots and a red striped shirt.

The film captured and expressed a part of the restaurant's soul. My grandparents reveled in the attention the film brought, with my grandfather wishing after the fact for a piece of the pie. True to character, he told Marty that he should have been paid a fee for letting him use Nepenthe in the film. My grandmother, on the other hand, told Marty business had at least doubled in the years following.

MAKES 18 TO 24 SMALL (BUT RICH) COOKIES

CRUST
¾ cup (1½ sticks) butter, room temperature
3 tablespoons granulated sugar
3 cups flour

FILLING
2 cups firmly packed brown sugar
3 eggs, beaten
3 tablespoons all-purpose flour
¾ teaspoon baking powder
1½ tablespoons pure vanilla extract
1½ cups chopped walnuts or pecans
¾ cup shredded unsweetened coconut

TOPPING
½ cup (1 stick) butter, room temperature
1½ cups confectioners' sugar, sifted
2 teaspoons pure vanilla extract
18 to 24 walnut or pecan halves (optional)

Passion Cookies

The beautiful Helen Weston, wife of Cole Weston (son of famed photographer Edward Weston), worked at Nepenthe in the early '60s and made these melt-in-your-mouth three-layer cookies for Richard Burton, who always asked for her to wait on him.

Preheat the oven to 350°F. Generously grease a 9 by 12-inch baking pan.

To make the crust, in a large bowl with a wooden spoon, beat the butter with the granulated sugar until creamy. Stir in the flour. Press evenly and firmly onto the bottom of the prepared pan. Bake for 20 minutes, until lightly golden.

To make the filling, cream the brown sugar and eggs in a mixing bowl. In a separate bowl, combine the flour with the baking powder, and mix into the sugar mixture. Stir in the vanilla, chopped walnuts, and coconut.

Pour the filling over the still-warm crust and spread evenly with a small offset spatula to cover. Return to the oven and bake for 20 minutes, until the filling is set. Cool completely on a rack.

To make the topping, mix the butter, confectioners' sugar, and vanilla in a mixing bowl until smooth. Thin with a little milk or cream if needed. Spread over the cooled cookies. Cut into small squares, as they are super rich. You can top each cookie with a nut half (as pictured) if desired.

CULTURE OF PLACE

Nepenthe was not always as gay and carefree as perceived, nor did my grandparents shy away from advancing their own agendas or providing the necessary space for others to deal with theirs. My grandmother, concerned about civil rights and wanting to do something for "the movement" in the early '60s, invited the novelist, playwright, and activist James Baldwin to come and speak. Unfortunately, he railed against Nepenthe and her guests, seeing it and company as a representation of the white bourgeois. My grandmother, terribly upset and disappointed, felt he never stopped to see that she was supportive of his ideals, as were her guests. By inviting him she hoped to give him a platform to speak his truth.

With the family's expanding enterprise and influx in business and tourism on the coast, my grandfather brought in a manager, Mary Belle Sheld (now Snow), to run the place in 1966. She worked six days a week that first year and lived on property with her young daughter, Tina. My grandfather would throw pebbles on her roof to get her attention if, after working the day shift, she wasn't back in the restaurant by 6:00 p.m.

At 9:00 p.m., "almost on the dot," my grandmother walked through the restaurant to make sure everything was in order—the director's chairs tucked just so, the pillows neatly lined up against the benches, the candles lit—a routine she followed for years. She watched the scene from her window above the terrace "surrounded by spools of yarn and reclining on the long beds with her notebooks," remembered Mary Belle.

She knew, instinctively, if something wasn't right. Once she got word that the Hell's Angels were coming into town, and she told Mary Belle to close the restaurant. When they arrived on the terrace, Mary Belle's job was to tell them that they were closed. My grandmother watched from the ramp above the terrace with her arms on her waist, not saying a word, until they left.

"Amazing, extraordinary things" happened at Nepenthe, Mary Belle stressed to me one evening during a marathon discussion about Nepenthe and the culture of place. She relayed the story about civil rights activist Dick Gregory the day Martin Luther King, Jr., died, April 4, 1968, as an example. Since we still didn't have a phone system in place, Gregory spent the afternoon on the pay phone next to the old office, making calls to every known political figure across the country. Staff and customers were stunned by the news and likewise amazed at Gregory's appearance there. The devastating repercussions of that day distinctively played themselves out, like many other instances, at the bottom of the ramp at the back door of Nepenthe.

CHAPTER 4

Lolly's Table

*oets, wanderers, seekers, [all] gathered around
her table where there was always plenty.*

—IRENE MASTELLER, FAMILY FRIEND

{ 4 }

LOLLY'S TABLE

My grandparents always fed people, even before they opened the restaurant. That was why they started Nepenthe in the first place, because they were forever entertaining large groups of friends and friends of friends, inviting people down for the day, the night, or longer. Friends from Carmel used to come on Thanksgiving Day and bring an already roasted turkey for a festive holiday picnic. They set up the Ping-Pong table in the restaurant and played long into the afternoon and evening. These early gatherings made way for merry holiday dinners in the restaurant that still go on today.

When traveling artists and musicians arrived from afar, my grandparents put them up, some for several months at a time, and the family table expanded ever wider. Once they took in two refugee brothers from Hungary; they lived and worked there and became a part of the family. During the building stages of the restaurant, they often fed the workers. The Trotter brothers, who built the restaurant, were favored guests, always telling wild stories recounting heroic feats of strength and eating copious amounts of food.

Originally private, Lolly's kitchen, or the "upstairs kitchen" as it was known throughout the community, was above the restaurant's main kitchen and attached to the log cabin. Open to a large extended crew of employees, family members, residents, visiting friends, and ultimately anyone in need, it fed upward of a hundred people at any given time, a little like a soup kitchen. It was also where my grandmother hosted her Sunday night dinners for her closest friends, where she orchestrated special events around the warmth of the sturdy family table, and where pianists and friends performed impromptu solos, on occasion also bursting into song. The family kitchen was known throughout the community as a place to share a warm meal and for the "kindness of Lolly."

My grandmother was an ample woman with a warm, generous spirit that permeated everyone's lives and provided a sense of security to many who knew her. I spent countless hours on her big bed, basking in her presence and affection. At times she taught me how to sew or crochet, and other times I took down notes for her, recorded the family history, or helped her respond to mail. I listened wide-eyed to her stories about living in Italy, the glorious food, the endless parties, and the picnics she had on the beach, among many other things.

As a child, I would bring my grandmother green apples from the walk-in and nestle into her large lap. She peeled them using a steak knife, then sliced them into wedges, placing the pieces in a small boat-shaped bowl. Sometimes I dipped them a bit of cinnamon and sugar. On occasion she'd try and peel the apple in one fell swoop and feed the snakelike peeling to me if I asked.

My grandmother delighted in a party and would go out of her way to make it special, whether making a certain food (or having it made for her), laying out a beautiful piece of fabric, or placing a bounty of wildflowers or plum blossoms in a gallon glass jar in the center of a table and adorning it with other festive items she had picked up in Chinatown. She liked things a little worn and that showed some texture and patina.

At age seventeen, like my grandmother, I went to Europe, where I spent four months with my French-Italian stepmother eating my way across the continent: couscous in Tunisia, wood-fired cooking in Italy, and ripe cheeses and country meals under a grape arbor in France.

While there, I gravitated to the family table, not unlike I imagine my grandmother did so many years before. Whether in the mountains in Italy or at a small vineyard property in the south of France with my stepmother's parents, every day was an invitation to gather around the table. When friends and family arrived they brought gifts of food: a special cheese from the region, fruit from their yard, or a jar of preserves they had made.

The family table became my sanctuary, the place where I felt most at home away from home. It was in the French farmhouse kitchen where I honed new skills, like butchering a chicken and rolling out homemade ravioli; in Italy where I witnessed the connection between farm and table; and in Tunisia where I experienced that sharing the gift of food could be as simple as sitting around a hearth in the desert with a cup of tea and a sweet. Food wasn't so much precious as it was an opportunity for giving. Like my grandmother's dinners, these experiences defined my relationship to food and reiterated the many ways it nourishes and sustains us.

Growing up, my two cousins, my older brother, Cap, and I bathed in my grandmother's bathroom or on the back porch in a wide, corner tub that we liked to think of as a swimming pool. We ate at the family table with all the employees and grouped in the living room on the long row of chenille-covered beds when it was time for a nap. We wandered throughout the grounds, invented projects in the maintenance shack, rambled through the garden and canyons, climbed the oak trees out front, made forts, and unabashedly spied on customers by appearing under their tables unexpectedly; we sometimes stole their french fries. We helped with construction projects, and once my grandmother bought us all pint-size wheelbarrows and our own shovels so that we could shovel sand into the mixer when they built the employee bathrooms.

During the holidays, we hammered tin cans to make shiny tree ornaments and pricked oranges with cloves for my grandmother's mulled wine until our fingers hurt. We decorated dozens of Easter

eggs in a vinegar solution or sometimes with a natural dye made from the skins of yellow onions. For Halloween we carved intricate designs into pumpkins and toasted the seeds for snacks. We occasionally climbed onto the roof to pick grapes, even though we weren't supposed to.

Like our parents, we grew up in the fury of restaurant life, with a mix of wonder and confusion. We toddled out to the terrace in early mornings in our pajamas, spent hours on my grandmother's big bed watching the customers below, and danced to entertain the guests. When we played make-believe we played "restaurant" because it was so much fun, jotting down our notes and pretending to name orders. Some of us made good use of the free box in the back parking lot, a community goodwill where people from all over Big Sur dropped off or helped themselves to books and clothing, or we raided my grandmother's costume wardrobes, occasionally carrying out homegrown productions on the terrace midday when it was full of customers. My children and their cousins have done the same thing.

There was always someone to play a game of chess or checkers with, or to take us to the beach, or into the hills. When my cousins and the children of employees showed up, we played kick the can in the back parking lot late into the night, or board games at the family kitchen table, or we huddled in my grandmother's living room to watch the one black-and-white TV.

PORTRAIT OF A FAMILY KITCHEN

Impressive in size, the family kitchen above the restaurant remained the hub of our extended family life. It connected to my grandmother's living room via a hallway crammed to the gills, once the original kitchen space in the log cabin. At one end of the family kitchen was a long, sturdy redwood table made by Guido, a sandal maker and local carpenter, where people gathered for lunch and dinner. Surrounded by a built-in bench and windows lined with colored wine bottles, it overlooked a small porch with a double bed for napping, and when we were very young, a corner pool for splashing and bathing. My grandmother sat in a wide fabric-covered armchair at the head of the table. An old upright piano stood behind the chair where anyone who knew how played on just about any occasion. Next to the piano was a stand-alone fireplace, along with another armchair where, on rainy afternoons, people napped or curled up with a book.

A small alcove off to one side with a built-in redwood closet was stuffed with costumes, copper platters, paintings, and games, and next to it was an ironing board where the staff ironed clothes for work. The closet's contents and everything on top spilled haphazardly into the large open kitchen space with its sturdy, square table for laying out the food, and a tin bread cupboard, chock-full of sliced breads, nailed to the beam next to it.

When I was growing up, the kitchen had peeling red Formica countertops, a commercial-sized, double-door stainless refrigerator, two stoves back to back (one a commercial Wolf range), and a funkier electric wall oven. There were two sinks in two locations. White generic cupboards with more counters running along another wall rounded out the space of mostly dark wood, as did a smattering of paintings, wine bottles, glass jars, and an Italian decorative fruit bowl of geese going around that was ever present. We stored our dry goods in a large walk-in pantry just off the kitchen by the refrigerator. At one time the pantry was my grandfather's office and featured a view of the coast.

A redwood, big-stoved, painting-hung kitchen overlooking the Pacific, it feeds, and sometimes houses, family, employees, people stranded by storm and accident, and members of the Big Sur community temporarily in need or "just visiting."

— *RECIPES FOR LIVING IN BIG SUR*

My aunts, uncles, and mother grew up at that family table, as did the next generation of my brother, Cap, and me, and cousins Kirk and Erin along with other cousins and extended family.

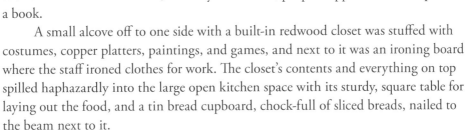

PUMPKIN SPICE CAKE
1 cup whole-wheat flour (not pastry flour)
1 cup unbleached white flour
1½ teaspoons baking soda
1 teaspoon cinnamon
½ teaspoon ground cloves
¼ teaspoon nutmeg
Pinch salt
1 cup vegetable oil
1½ cups brown sugar, firmly packed
2 eggs
2 teaspoons pure vanilla extract
1 (15-ounce) can pumpkin puree (about 1¾ cups)
¼ cup molasses
¾ cup raisins
½ cup walnuts, coarsely chopped

SOUR CREAM FROSTING
½ cup (4 ounces) cream cheese, softened
½ cup sour cream
1 teaspoon pure vanilla extract
About 2 cups confectioners' sugar

Pumpkin Spice Cake (Bohemian Wedding Cake)

My grandmother came up with Nepenthe's pumpkin spice cake for her son Griff's wedding to his wife, Rosalyn, in 1960. By running out of one ingredient and substituting another, adding in a little whole-wheat flour and other flavorings, she declared it a "Bohemian wedding cake," said my aunt Dorcas, who helped make it.

This dense, very moist cake is loaded with nuts and raisins and comes out a deep, chocolate brown. My aunt Rosalyn sent me my grandmother's original handwritten recipe, calling for less sugar and eggs than we use today, and for oleo or butter (it makes a dense, more earthy cake) rather than oil. As a matter of taste, the cake is quite good either way.

Preheat the oven to 350°F. Lightly butter and flour a 9-inch round cake pan, knocking out any excess flour.

For the cake, combine the whole-wheat flour, white flour, baking soda, cinnamon, cloves, nutmeg, and salt in a medium bowl. In a large bowl, stir together the oil and brown sugar, mixing well. Beat in the eggs, one at a time. Stir in the vanilla. Mix in the pumpkin puree and then the molasses. Stir in the dry ingredients, mixing until thoroughly incorporated. Stir in the raisins and walnuts.

Pour the batter into the prepared pan. Bake about 1 hour, until a toothpick inserted in the middle comes out clean. Cool on a rack for 15 minutes, then invert and cool completely.

For the frosting, mix the cream cheese, sour cream, and vanilla in a medium bowl until smooth. Sift in the confectioners' sugar and mix well. It should be thinner than a typical cream cheese frosting.

Place the cake on a cake plate. Spread a thin layer of frosting on top and all over the side. Freeze any leftover frosting, or reserve for muffins or cupcakes.

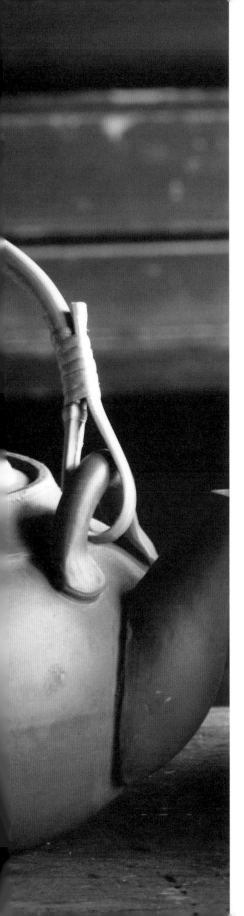

Butter and Radish Sandwiches

My grandmother taught me how to make tea (or finger) sandwiches one afternoon, as we stood side-by-side at the worn Formica counter. I was both surprised and delighted at what they actually were, just enough of something to delight the eyes and pleasure the mouth at the same time.

Slice half a sweet baguette thinly into rounds. Have ready a stick of European-style sweet butter at room temperature, a pinch dish of sea salt, and a bunch of French breakfast radishes crisping in water, as well as some just-picked parsley or chervil. If it happens that the radish leaves are fresh and in good condition, cut them into thin slivers as garnish, or leave whole to adorn the plate.

Spread each baguette round with some of the butter, thick enough that you know it's there. Sprinkle with some of the salt and top with a few slices of radish and a minute snip of parsley or chervil, if desired. Arrange on a plate and serve as a late afternoon snack or with drinks before dinner.

Italian Rusks

My grandmother loved to make rusks, toasty crusts of twice-baked bread that she served with jam and honey. She kept them in a tin can in the living room for easy snacking. When friends came to visit in the afternoons, she poured smoky Chinese black tea (lapsang souchong) to serve with the rusks. I imagine she had her first taste of these twice-baked breads in Italy.

Choose sliced day-old bread with good flavor and structure, such as rye or seeded loaves flavored with anise or caraway. Lay slices on baking sheets. Bake in a 275°F oven for 2 hours or longer, until crisp and quite hard. Store in a tin.

MAKES ABOUT 12 HOTCAKES, SERVING 4

½ cup white unbleached flour
½ cup whole-wheat flour
2 tablespoons wheat germ
1 teaspoon baking powder
½ teaspoon baking soda
Pinch sugar, or a drop of maple syrup (optional)
Pinch ground flaxseed (optional)
Pinch salt
1 egg
2 tablespoons canola oil, plus more for cooking
¾ to 1 cup buttermilk or milk
2 heaping tablespoons cottage cheese, sour cream, or yogurt

Lolly's Famous Hotcakes

My grandmother became famous up and down the coast for her sour cream pancakes, big batches thrown together for a crowd without a recipe. She started with a base of Bisquick, to which she added eggs, soured milk or sour cream, and just about everything else except the kitchen sink, including whole-wheat flour, rice, cottage cheese, applesauce, or corn. They were either very fluffy or thin with crisped edges.

My aunt Holly picked up where she left off, making her own mix and adding flaxseed. One of her tricks is that she never quite lets the batter run out, adding to it each day, so that it has built up a sourdough-like flavor over time. If using milk instead of buttermilk, omit the baking soda.

In a large bowl, mix the white flour, whole-wheat flour, wheat germ, baking powder, baking soda, sugar, flaxseed, and salt. Mix the egg with the oil in a smaller bowl and add to the dry ingredients. Stir in ¾ cup buttermilk and the cottage cheese until just moistened. The batter should be slightly thick, even a little lumpy, but still pourable. Add more buttermilk as needed.

Heat a cast-iron skillet with a little oil, or spray with a nonstick cooking spray. When hot, pour spoonfuls of batter into the pan, making a few pancakes at a time. When air bubbles form on the surface of the cakes, flip and cook for another minute or so, until done. Repeat with the remaining batter. Top with butter and maple syrup.

SERVES 4 TO 6

1¼ pounds boneless lamb (shoulder or leg), cubed
1½ tablespoons curry powder
1½ tablespoons flour
2 teaspoons salt
1 teaspoon cumin seed, toasted and ground,
    or 1½ teaspoons ground cumin
1 teaspoon freshly ground black pepper
2 tablespoons vegetable oil
1 large onion, chopped
2 cloves garlic, finely chopped
2 teaspoons dried thyme
1 dried red chile pepper
1 bay leaf
2 tablespoons tomato paste
3 cups water
1 green apple, peeled, cored, and chopped
¼ fresh pineapple, peeled, cored, and diced
½ cup shredded unsweetened coconut
½ cup raisins
¾ to 1 cup coconut milk
Red pepper flakes (optional)

Lolly's Lamb Curry

My grandmother's sweet and tangy curry was a family favorite and originally published in *Recipes for Living in Big Sur*. I have given it a slight update, included measurements, and added chile for spice. Serve with Lolly's Oven-Baked Rice (page 152).

Dust the lamb with the curry powder, flour, salt, cumin, and black pepper. Toss, using your hands, to thoroughly coat. Heat 1 tablespoon of the oil in a wide, heavy bottomed large pot. Add the lamb and cook, stirring and scraping up the browned bits as the meat cooks, until browned on all sides, about 5 minutes. Transfer the lamb to a bowl.

Heat the remaining 1 tablespoon oil in the same pot. Add the onion and cook until translucent. Add the garlic, thyme, chile, and bay leaf and cook for 1 minute. Stir in the tomato paste and water. Add the apple, pineapple, coconut, raisins, and browned lamb. Bring to a boil and boil for 2 minutes. Reduce the heat and gently simmer, stirring occasionally, for about 1 hour, until the flavors meld.

Stir in the coconut milk and continue simmering for 20 to 30 minutes, until the lamb is cooked through. The curry should be slightly thick and saucy. Add a little coconut milk to thin, as needed. Discard the bay leaf and chile pepper before serving.

In the Family Kitchen

Family kitchen meals were simple, laid out on a square oak table in the middle of the kitchen. For lunch, the cooks set out sliced meats and cheese and platters of fixings for sandwiches along with deviled eggs, celery sticks, carrots, sliced tomatoes, and olives. For dinner, it was big bowls of pasta primavera, or pasta with pesto or a hearty meat sauce; perhaps a roast or a meat loaf along with fruit, nuts, and large bowls of greens. Some days the cook made food to order, standing in front of the Wolf range and flipping omelets and frying ham and potatoes for a late breakfast.

We loved it when my grandmother came in and whipped up a batch of her hotcakes with corn, or grated leftover baked potatoes to make crisp potato pancakes, smearing them with a bit of sour cream and sprinkling with chives. Or when the bakers baked homemade bread or rich brownies for an afternoon treat. If we were lucky we could sneak into the restaurant to have ice cream for dessert, mixing all three flavors in a creamer tin and sitting on the bleachers watching the world go by. Occasionally the ice cream man would leave us our favorite flavor studded with marshmallows and toasted almond (Rocky Road).

Family dinners were typically homey roasts, baked fish, layered casseroles, big pots of Spanish rice, or an ethnic stew. It was food easily prepared for a crowd; comfort food that was unpretentious, hearty, and made with love. There was the occasional grumpy family cook, but we managed to have a good time. Food was abundant and you could eat as much as you wanted, including Dagwood-sized sandwiches and slices of lasagna as large as a house. It was a good gig for the people who worked there.

I can easily recall the aroma of hearty pot roasts wafting through the family kitchen and out the door, or her vegetable gratin with a golden, crusty edge of cheese.

Nani and Lolly

SERVES 4

½ pound fresh chanterelle mushrooms
1½ tablespoons olive oil
3 tablespoons butter
1 large shallot or small onion, finely chopped
2 cloves garlic, minced
2 sprigs fresh thyme, stemmed
⅔ cup vegetable stock or water
Salt and freshly ground black pepper
8 to 12 ounces dried pappardelle pasta or other wide pasta
2 tablespoons chopped fresh parsley
Zest of 1 lemon
¼ cup grated Parmesan cheese, plus more for passing

Pappardelle with Chanterelles

Come chanterelle season, it was almost a given that someone from the community would arrive at my grandmother's kitchen after a day of foraging and unload pounds of the aromatic mushrooms onto the counter, prompting a feast. A heaping bowl of sautéed chanterelles with pasta and lots of parsley was a familiar favorite. Considered gold by the culinary world, found chanterelles were a regular part of my grandmother's Sunday night dinners and were often featured in the Thanksgiving meal.

Gently clean the mushrooms with a dry brush. Avoid soaking in water. Trim any dry stems. Slice the mushrooms into ½-inch pieces.

Heat the oil and 1 tablespoon of the butter in a large heavy skillet over medium-high heat. Add the shallot and cook for 1 minute. Stir in the mushrooms, garlic, and thyme and sauté until the mushrooms are browned, 3 to 5 minutes. Ladle in the stock, season with salt and pepper, and simmer for 3 minutes, until the mushrooms are just tender. Remove from the heat.

Meanwhile, cook the pasta in boiling salted water until al dente. Reserve ½ cup of the pasta water and then drain the pasta in a colander. Add the pasta to the mushrooms in the skillet along with the remaining 2 tablespoons of the butter. Cook over moderately high heat, tossing the pasta to coat and adding pasta water to moisten if needed, until thoroughly coated. Stir in the parsley and lemon zest. Divide the pasta among 4 warm plates and sprinkle with the Parmesan. Pass additional Parmesan separately.

SERVES 4 TO 6

TOMATO SAUCE
1 tablespoon olive oil
1 or 2 cloves garlic, finely chopped
1 (14-ounce) can plum tomatoes, preferably San Marzano, with juice
1 sprig fresh rosemary
1 tablespoon water
Salt and freshly ground black pepper

4 to 5 medium zucchini
Salt and freshly ground black pepper
3 to 4 tablespoons olive oil
1 onion, halved and thinly sliced
2 teaspoons chopped fresh thyme
1/3 cup fresh bread crumbs, preferably homemade
1 tablespoon chopped fresh parsley
½ to ¾ cup grated Parmesan cheese

Zucchini Parmesan

This hearty Italian casserole brings back vivid memories of my grandmother standing at the stove, frying thick slabs of zucchini or rounds of salted eggplant, her ample frame leaning heavy into the Wolf range. She made this dish often, layering vegetables randomly in a commercial-sized roasting pan and topping them with a coarse tomato sauce and lots of cheese.

I have replicated it to the best of my memory, taking liberties with the ingredients, like adding homemade bread crumbs and making my own tomato sauce. Serve as a side dish to meat or fish, or accompanied by a salad as a main.

Preheat the oven to 375°F.

For the tomato sauce, heat the olive oil in a skillet over medium-high heat. Add the garlic, whole tomatoes with juice, and rosemary. Gently crush the tomatoes with the back of a wooden spoon. Swirl the water in the can to pick up the last of the tomato juices and add to the pan. Decrease the heat and gently simmer for 15 to 20 minutes, until thick and jamlike. Season to taste with salt and pepper. Discard the rosemary sprig. The sauce can be made ahead, stored in the refrigerator for up to 4 days, and reheated before using.

Trim the zucchini and slice lengthwise into 4 or 5 ribbons each. Season with salt and pepper. Heat 1 or 2 tablespoons olive oil in a large skillet or cast-iron pan. Add the zucchini, in batches if necessary, and fry until browned on both sides. Transfer to a paper towel–lined plate to soak up some of the oil. Cut each piece in half, crosswise.

In a separate skillet, heat 1 tablespoon olive oil over medium heat. Add the onion and thyme and cook, stirring occasionally, until translucent and just beginning to brown, about 10 minutes. Season with salt; transfer to a small bowl.

In the same skillet, heat 2 teaspoons oil over low heat. Stir in the bread crumbs and cook until golden, 2 to 3 minutes. Remove from the heat and stir in the parsley.

Arrange the zucchini in a 2-quart baking dish, overlapping the slices to make one dense layer. Top with the onion mixture and cover with the tomato sauce. Sprinkle with the cheese, then with the bread crumbs. Cover tightly with aluminum foil. Bake until bubbling, about 45 minutes. Remove the foil and bake for 5 to 10 minutes longer, until golden brown on top.

Oven-Baked Rice

"Perfect rice every time with no attention."

Preheat the oven to 375°F. For every cupful of rice, either brown or white, use 1 ½ cups water. Place in a baking dish, add a knob of butter if desired, and cover tightly with foil. Bake for 45 to 60 minutes, until the rice is tender and the liquid is absorbed. Fluff with a fork before serving.

SUNDAY NIGHT DINNERS

Sunday night dinners reflected my grandmother's passion for conversation, food, the arts, and a spirited bohemian lifestyle. The guests were a cast of her dearest and oldest friends, mostly creative types who were as drawn to Big Sur's beauty and unconventional way of life as she was. Dinners were intimate but informal, held at the long, sturdy redwood table at the far corner of the family kitchen. The evenings usually ended in her living room, where everyone gathered to watch one of two channels on an old black-and-white television.

These gatherings were in many ways theatrical affairs, with sporadic poetry readings and guests occasionally arriving in costume. My grandmother always

Barbara and Doug

wore a Chinese-style waist-length tunic with a mandarin collar that she had made for her, her hair swooped into a chignon and wrapped in a chic, red scarf. Lewis Perkins, "Oodie" to his friends, an actor from the Pasadena Playhouse, came in polka-dot palazzo pants and flamboyant shirts. Her longtime friend Douglas Madsen occasionally arrived ceremoniously in top hat and tails astride a black stallion, his lover next to him on a white horse. At the table, he told stories about meeting my grandmother as a young woman on the island of Capri, more than forty years before, and about how she danced with Mussolini. Russian artist Amelia Newell, former wife of sculptor Gordon Newell, arrived no less dramatically in flowing caftans, her neck draped with multiple garlands of thick beads.

My grandmother's dinners were never really as much about the food as they were about the gathering of people. Food was simple and comforting. She just threw things together, a little of this or that, and then popped it into the oven, remembered one friend. It was as if she was perpetually celebrating her capacity to feed a crowd. "It was not a dozen eggs, but a case of eggs," my uncle Griff said of how she cooked, all with a distinctive panache.

A typical dinner might include a vegetable gratin, roasted root vegetables, or thinly sliced potatoes baked in cream until the edges were crisped and golden, a baked fish or a pork roast, and a salad. I loved her salads: tart, salty, and tossed at the last minute with olive oil and fresh lemon juice. She served red wine in carafes and set the food in the center of the table to be passed family style. Friends arrived from Carmel and as far away as Los Angeles and usually brought something to share. Stefano Cacace, an Italian gardener friend, brought his rose pie (a decorative centerpiece) and Barbara Woyt, local baker and frequent guest, often brought her homemade bread.

SERVES 4

4 (6-ounce) fillets white fish, such as cod,
    sablefish, or snapper
Salt and freshly ground black pepper
1 lemon, thinly sliced
2 or 3 sprigs fresh marjoram, stemmed and coarsely chopped
Handful of cherry tomatoes, or 4 quartered plum tomatoes
2 tablespoons olive oil
⅓ to ½ cup dry white wine

Baked Fish with Marjoram

My grandmother made cooking a whole fish look easy, slapping it in a pan with a generous helping of herbs, tomatoes, and wine. At home, I prepare fish similarly, but rarely do I cook it whole, instead purchasing fillets or the occasional half side. Wild cod is a Pacific coast fish often caught locally, but any white fish will do, such as snapper or sablefish. Serve with steamed new potatoes drizzled with warm butter.

Preheat the oven to 375°F.

Season the fish with salt and pepper and place it in a baking dish. Scatter around the lemon, marjoram, and tomatoes. Gently crush the tomatoes with the back of a spoon. Drizzle the fish with the olive oil and pour over the wine.

Cover tightly with aluminum foil. Bake for about 15 minutes, until the fish flakes easily with a fork. Serve with the lemon slices, tomatoes, and pan juices.

How I marveled at her handling of a whole fish—slapping it into a commercial-sized pan, adding fresh herbs and tomatoes, then drizzling it with olive oil before popping it into the oven and retiring to her room while it cooked.

*M*y grandmother's culinary prowess grew not at all from what she cooked, but from the generosity of her meals and the invitation to join her and the family around the table. That sharing food was less about the perfect spread (though it was always good) and instead about the gathering is no surprise, based on her years in Europe and the lifestyle that she embraced—and in her way, tried to emulate at Nepenthe, if not in her life.

As the demands of the restaurant grew and the family kitchen fed more people, cooking at times became a chore. Nevertheless, the family kitchen plugged along, and the getting together around the table stayed constant. To this day, it is one of our lasting legacies, whether the family comes together at the restaurant, with all three generations practically spilling out of our chairs and onto the terrace, or at my aunt's house around the same family table where we grew up. We also share a big feast on Thanksgiving and Christmas with staff, their families, and a host of friends. Food is the antidote to what ails us in times of struggle and separation, bringing us back to the table, back into each other's lives.

Recipes from my family kitchen are a taste of what draws me back home. They speak to family and cooking that is simple, straightforward, and created with heart.

1 head escarole
1 small head curly endive (chicory) or frisée
1 head butter lettuce, such as Bibb or Boston lettuce
1 head radicchio, such as Early Treviso or Chioggia
2 cloves garlic, smashed
Sea salt
Juice of 2 or 3 lemons
Balsamic vinegar (optional)
Olive oil
Freshly ground black pepper
Parmesan cheese, for shaving (optional)

Chicory Salad with Lemon and Olive Oil

For years, Nepenthe garnished its dinner plates with thick stalks of curly endive (also known as chicory), considered a digestive in Italy but little used or known here. Favored by my grandmother, she added it to her salads, dressing it with lots of garlic, lemon, and olive oil, and likewise ate it plain.

I like to mix it with other greens from the same family, like radicchio and escarole, and then add a milder lettuce, like a butter leaf. Young dandelion greens also go well within this mix. Look for smaller heads of chicory, as they tend to be less bitter, or use only the inner leaves. Shave Parmesan over the top, as here, or toss in some homemade croutons for contrast.

Trim the ends of the escarole and endive, discarding any tough outer leaves (or reserve for braising). Rinse in cool water and pat dry on a towel. Separate the butter lettuce leaves, rinse, and pat dry. Tear the greens into smaller pieces.

Cut the base of the radicchio and separate the leaves. Rinse and pat try. Tear some of the larger outer leaves into smaller pieces, leaving the smaller ones whole.

In the bottom of a large, wooden salad bowl, using the tines of a fork, mash the garlic cloves with a healthy pinch of salt to make a paste. Add the lemon juice and a drop of vinegar. Whisk in enough olive oil, about ⅓ to ½ cup, to make a balanced dressing. Add lots of freshly ground black pepper. Add the salad greens to the bowl and toss to coat. Shave Parmesan over top.

Thanksgiving

During my childhood, the huge Thanksgiving dinners at Nepenthe happened pretty much by volunteer effort. My grandmother had a group of close friends she relied on, often the same few people year after year, who cooked, cleaned, and were pretty much responsible for the whole affair. In a way, their efforts made it such a unique event, drawing on Nepenthe's history as an artists' enclave and fueled my grandmother's inclination to give back to people. "She did it for the community," my aunt Dorcas told me, and it was very important to her. The tradition has continued at Nepenthe, which feeds over a hundred people on Thanksgiving night. In some years, almost half as many more extended family members join in the festivities.

Thanksgiving is my favorite time to return home. It is the holiday most often filled with family arriving from far off, when all of the cousins and siblings see each other, and likewise the next generation of grandkids reconnects. This is when the games of our youth resurface, like tag and kick the can in the parking lot, and when the kids explore the lower garden, making swords from tree limbs, or chasing each other down the windy trail toward the beach. From the restaurant, we sometimes hear their joyful cries as they run unfettered through the canyon.

By midday the family kitchen is bustling with cooks. My grandmother was at the helm when she was alive, ordering us kids from her living room to do this or that: collect the potatoes, gather flowers for decoration, and so forth. My aunt Holly still bakes the desserts for this day and I often help. By noon the pies have already been baked and the ovens are full of turkeys, timed to come out about an hour before service. Robin Burnside (formerly Wilson), who was very close to my grandmother and ran Nepenthe's Café Amphora for close to ten years with her then-husband, reminded me how my grandmother would come out of her living room just before service to make her giblet gravy, the pièce de résistance of the meal. The last year before she died, she called Robin into the living room and asked her to make the gravy, and Robin knew then that she really wasn't well.

Then as now, multiple turkeys are roasted in oversize metal pans, and pounds of potatoes and vegetables are trimmed and prepared for dinner. In the old days we draped the turkeys with white towels dipped in butter and (believe it or not) Crisco to keep the meat moist. We made mashed potatoes by the vat and that typical, sticky-sweet '70s dish of yams with marshmallows cooked to a golden brown. We set out large platters of steamed green beans drizzled with nutty browned butter, soft dinner rolls, a winter greens salad tossed in a large pottery bowl, creamed onions, and cranberry sauce. It was typical holiday fare in an untypical setting. Guests often brought dishes to share, favorite casseroles and homemade pies and cookies and sometimes tins of candies put out amid the jumble of food. And then there was always turkey soup the next day, and thick slices of leftover bird for sandwiches to take with us to the beach.

William, Sumner, Nicoya, and Chama

MAKES ABOUT 3½ CUPS

5 tablespoons flour
¼ cup fat skimmed from the turkey roasting pan, or butter
2 or 3 tablespoons brandy or wine (optional), plus pan juices
Rich turkey stock, heated
Reserved giblets, neck, and any other bits and pieces
    from the turkey, chopped
Salt and freshly ground black pepper
Fresh sage or other herbs (optional)
2 tablespoons chilled cream or milk

Lolly's Giblet Gravy

Making good gravy is an art, but my grandmother made it look easy. She approached it as she did most everything, with confidence and verve. When you saw her at the stove on Thanksgiving night, whisk in hand, it was a sign that dinner was about to start. As if on cue, her kitchen mice would go scrambling, rushing the covered platters of succulent turkey and all the trimmings from the family kitchen down to the restaurant for service.

I don't think she had much of a formula, just a good sense of what she was doing and a knack for getting it right. So, while I offer measurements and a slightly different method, it's still straightforward. Don't forget to reserve the fat and juices from your roasted turkey—and don't throw out those giblets.

Toast the flour in a dry small skillet over low heat, shaking and stirring for a minute or two until it is lightly browned; set aside. Skim the fat from the turkey drippings and reserve. Deglaze the roasting pan with a little brandy or wine (or stock), scraping up any dark bits to incorporate. Pour into a measuring cup and add enough hot stock to equal 4 cups.

In the deglazed roasting pan or a wide heavy skillet, heat the fat over medium-high heat. Sprinkle with the toasted flour and stir to incorporate. Cook for 2 minutes. Gradually whisk in the 4 cups of hot stock. Simmer for 15 to 20 minutes, or longer to burn off any flour taste, until the gravy coats the back of a spoon. Add more stock as needed. Stir in the chopped giblets and turkey bits and season to taste with salt and pepper and sage or other aromatics. Whisk in the cold cream to finish, and simmer 1 minute.

VARIATION: To make my grandmother's chanterelle gravy, sauté 3 cups sliced chanterelles (about 12 ounces) in a little butter with some shallots and garlic. Stir into the gravy along with the giblets.

SERVES 6 TO 8

1 cup whole milk
⅔ cup heavy cream
1 clove garlic, peeled
1 sprig fresh thyme
Dash grated fresh nutmeg
2 pounds sweet potatoes, preferably garnet yams, peeled
1 pound Yukon Gold or Yellow Finn potatoes, scrubbed
2 tablespoons butter, plus more for buttering the dish
Salt and freshly ground black pepper
¾ cup grated Gruyère cheese
¼ cup freshly grated Parmesan cheese
1 or 2 tablespoons chopped fresh thyme

Sweet Potato Gratin

Here is a more elegant version of my grandmother's cheesy potato bake, and yet it is as simple to make. Serve alongside any main course, or on its own with a brightly dressed salad to counterpoint the richness of the cream.

Preheat the oven to 375°F. Lightly butter a medium gratin dish.

In a medium saucepan, combine the milk, cream, garlic, thyme sprig, and nutmeg and heat to just under a boil. Remove from the heat, cover, and steep for 10 minutes. Strain.

Thinly slice the sweet potatoes, using a mandolin or a very sharp knife. Similarly slice the unpeeled Yukon Gold potatoes. Layer half of each in the prepared gratin dish, gently pressing down as you go. Dot with 1 tablespoon butter and season with salt and pepper. Sprinkle with half the Gruyère, half the Parmesan, and half the thyme. Repeat with the remaining potatoes, butter, herbs, salt and pepper, and cheeses. Pour the cream mixture over the top.

Cover tightly with aluminum foil and bake for 50 minutes. Uncover, increase the temperature to 400°F, and continue baking for 15 to 20 minutes, until the potatoes are cooked through and the top is golden. Let sit 5 minutes before serving.

1¾ cups pumpkin puree (about a 15-ounce can)
¾ cup sugar
1 teaspoon cinnamon
½ teaspoon ground ginger
¼ teaspoon ground cloves
½ teaspoon salt
2 eggs
¾ cup heavy cream, or half and half
1 tablespoon pure vanilla extract
½ recipe Holly's Pie Dough (page 292)

Holly's Pumpkin Pie

My aunt makes her tried and true pumpkin pie each year to raves. Ironically, her recipe originated from the back of a Libby's pumpkin can, but she adds pure vanilla extract, measured by the capful, to make it her own. For the record, I've substituted heavy cream or half and half, and less of it, for the canned milk she uses, a personal preference. Top the pie with dollops of chantilly cream, if you like.

Pumpkin puree can be made fresh by roasting a sugar pumpkin, scooping out the flesh, pureeing it, and draining it in cheesecloth to release extra liquid.

Preheat the oven to 350°F.

For the pie, combine the pumpkin puree, sugar, cinnamon, ginger, cloves, and salt in a large bowl. Whisk in the eggs and cream. Stir in the vanilla.

Roll out the pie dough and fit into a 9-inch pie pan. Flute the edges.

Pour the filling into the pie shell. Bake until the filling is set, about 30 minutes.

Cool the pie for at least 30 minutes, then chill before serving.

Christmas

The minute school got out for the holidays, we began preparations for the annual Christmas feast, a week of pulling boxes of shiny ornaments from hidden nooks, dusting off the old Kilim rugs for display, and waiting eagerly for family and friends to show up from far away. We placed a tall tree in the center of the restaurant (and still do), decorating it on the morning of my aunt Holly's birthday, December 22. On Christmas Day at the restaurant we serve Lolly's Roast Chicken (page 113), then close for the evening. That night we share a meal with family, staff, and friends, once prepared by my grandmother and cast, and today, by my cousin Erin's husband, Tom.

We kids helped cook for the annual feast, collected redwood branches and other natural decorations for the tables, made ornaments, and spent hours pricking cloves into bright oranges and lemons for my grandmother's mulled wine, our fingers bruised and tired by the end. For ornaments, we hammered the backs of tin-can lids that my grandmother saved throughout the year, pounding them against a thick trunk of redwood reserved for this purpose. The indentations made by the round of the hammer catch the light beautifully.

The family picked out a tree from the canyon. Invariably, it would be tall and almost hit the ceiling, misshapen but wonderfully so, with lots of space between the branches to showcase the shiny ornaments. We placed the tree on a round table in the center of the restaurant, draping it with antique beads, shiny balls, and the gold lids. Today, Nepenthe purchases a tree from a tree lot, placing it on one of the smaller four-tops up front to leave more room for dining; it is no less festive and still adorned with family heirlooms. Recently my uncle Kaffe sent a boxful of fabric-covered fans he made to decorate a tree at the Victoria and Albert Museum in London. The fans, in an array of colors and patterns of his design, cast the tree in an Asian light, something my grandmother would have loved.

My grandmother put up another tree in her living room. She placed it at the center of the heavy chest that is still in the cabin, wrapped the tree base in colored burlap, and similarly decorated it with strands of beads and the shimmering tin lids. She hung her ornaments with colored yarn and tucked little treasures, like miniature dollhouse pieces and china dolls with hand-knit clothes, underneath. Piles of things around the tree included a collection of fabrics, presents wrapped in red flannel, and sweet things, like German licorice, amaretti cookies, and chocolate, often unwrapped, tucked under the branches.

Something I cherish around the holidays is to return to my grandmother's living room to have tea with my cousin and our children. There, we make holiday cards, paint, and wrap presents, the kids darting to and from my aunt's house across the highway. Below the cabin, the restaurant is a flurry of activity as old friends and other family members make holiday appearances. Meanwhile, the heavy door of the cabin opens and closes all day, sending a quick draft of cold wind into the room now heated by the cast-iron stove sitting in the old stone hearth. Like my grandmother, Erin places their tree on the large trunk and decorates it with the tin lids and other trinkets. She fills the trunk surface with gifts wrapped in fabric and brown paper she stamps with gold and silver paint. The tree shimmers and reflects beautifully in the large oval gold-rimmed mirror on the wall behind it, just as it did when my grandmother lived there.

SERVES 4 TO 6

12 whole cloves
1 orange
½ cup water
½ cup granulated sugar
1 cinnamon stick
½ vanilla bean
3 slices lemon peel
1 (750-milliliter) bottle fruity red wine
Brandy (optional)

Mulled Wine

Every Christmas at Nepenthe we made mulled wine and served it out of a copper teakettle at the start of dinner. The kids' job was to push the cloves into the oranges and lemons in the days before. I remember sitting around my grandmother's table with a big bowl of brightly colored fruit and a pile of the pointed cloves, whining about the task and how our fingers hurt. She would be happy to know that the family does it without complaining now.

Unlike in some recipes, my grandmother simmered her mulled wine for a long time, adding more wine as it reduced. The hours-long process filled the cabin with a sweet, spicy fragrance all afternoon. I like to add a vanilla bean to mine, and finish with a little brandy. One orange with plenty of cloves should do the trick for up to two bottles of wine. I use the peel of lemon only.

Stick the cloves into the orange, making a decorative pattern if you like.

Combine the orange, water, sugar, cinnamon, vanilla bean, and lemon peel in a large, nonreactive pot and simmer for 10 minutes. Pour in the wine. Simmer over low heat until the flavors meld, about 30 minutes. Just before serving, pour in a jigger or two of brandy. Serve hot.

CHRISTMAS
JUG
Put your name in
Pull a Name out

About 10 fresh sage leaves
3 sprigs fresh rosemary, stemmed and coarsely chopped
4 to 6 cloves garlic, finely chopped
1 tablespoon salt
⅓ cup plus 2 tablespoons olive oil
1 (2½ to 3-pound) pork loin roast, butterflied
Freshly ground black pepper
Wine-Poached Quince with Rosemary (recipe follows)
8 to 10 small new potatoes, scrubbed and halved
1 large onion, coarsely chopped
2 carrots, peeled and coarsely chopped
Salt
Chopped fresh thyme or rosemary

Herb-Stuffed Pork Loin Roast with Wine-Poached Quince

This is a nod to my grandmother's crown pork roast with apricots, a long-ago family favorite served for special occasions. In the absence of quince, you can poach plums or apples, or serve the pork simply with just the potatoes and vegetables.

Have your butcher butterfly the pork loin. You can stuff it and roll it up to a day ahead. This is also a great next-day dish, the pork wrapped in foil and slowly reheated or served cold, slices of it stuffed in a baguette with wedges of quince as a tasty sandwich.

Coarsely chop 5 of the sage leaves. Combine with the rosemary, garlic, and salt in a small bowl. Slowly whisk in the ⅓ cup oil to make a paste.

Open up the pork loin on a clean surface (or, if preparing ahead, leave on the butcher paper and wrap the paper back around it after it is stuffed and tied). Rub the herb paste all over the top and season with black pepper. Roll up the loin, starting with the end that has the least exterior fat (you want the fat end to be on the outside). Tie in 5 or 6 places, using butcher's twine, and tuck a whole sage leaf under each band. Place the loin in a baking dish, cover, and refrigerate for 2 hours.

Meanwhile, prepare the quince (page 174). This can also be done up to several days ahead, and brought to room temperature or warmed to serve.

About 30 minutes before you are ready to cook the pork, remove it from the refrigerator. Preheat the oven to 350°F.

Surround the pork with the potatoes, onion, and carrots. Drizzle with the remaining 2 tablespoons olive oil and season liberally with salt, pepper, and chopped thyme.

Roast for 1 hour or longer, occasionally basting with the drippings, until the juices run clear when the center of the pork is pricked with a skewer or the internal temperature is at least 145°F for medium, or depending on how well cooked you like it. The temperature will rise 10 degrees or so as it sits, so adjust accordingly. Transfer to a serving platter, leaving the vegetables in the pan. Cover the pork loosely with foil and allow it to rest for 10 to 15 minutes before slicing.

Raise the oven temperature to 400°F. Give the vegetables a good stir. (If there is an excess of juices, pour off into a small saucepot, skimming the fat, and boil for 3 to 5 minutes to reduce, saving for service.) Return the vegetables to the oven and cook until the potatoes are golden, about 10 minutes.

Thinly slice the pork roast. Serve with the pan juices, poached quince, and vegetables.

MAKES ABOUT 2 CUPS

2 medium quince
Peel of ½ lemon
1¼ cups water
1 cup dry white wine
⅓ cup honey
4 tablespoons granulated sugar
1 bay leaf
1 sprig fresh rosemary
½ cinnamon stick
2 black peppercorns

Wine-Poached Quince with Rosemary

Peel and core the quince. Slice into thin wedges and drop into a bowl of lemon water.

Combine the lemon peels, the 1¼ cups water, the wine, honey, sugar, bay leaf, rosemary, cinnamon, and peppercorns in a medium saucepan. Bring to a boil then decrease the heat to medium. Drain the quince and add it to the poaching liquid. Press a small round of parchment paper onto the quince to keep them submerged in liquid. Simmer until the quince are fork tender, 30 to 40 minutes. Transfer the quince to a small bowl. Return the liquid to a boil. Boil until thick and syrupy, 3 to 5 minutes. Pour over the quince and let cool.

MAKES 1 (9-INCH) CAKE, SERVING 8 TO 10

2 cups persimmon puree
¾ cup granulated sugar
¾ cup whole milk
½ cup (1 stick) butter, melted
½ cup whipping cream
¼ cup honey
3 eggs
2 tablespoons brandy (optional)
1½ cups flour
1 teaspoon baking soda
1 teaspoon baking powder
1 teaspoon cinnamon
1 teaspoon ground ginger
½ teaspoon freshly grated nutmeg
Scant ½ teaspoon ground cloves
½ teaspoon salt
1 cup toasted walnuts (optional)

Persimmon Pudding Cake

This was a favorite dessert of my grandmother's. I used to baked multiple batches of it in emptied coffee tins for holiday gifts. More pudding-like than cake, it should be served with a brandy hard sauce or softly whipped, lightly sweetened cream.

Use 4 or 5 ripe Hachiya (acorn-shaped) persimmons for the puree. Slice them open, scoop out the flesh, and push the pulp through a sieve to remove any seeds.

Preheat the oven to 375°F. Lightly grease a 9-inch baking dish or smaller individual molds.

In a large bowl, whisk together the puree, sugar, milk, butter, cream, honey, and eggs until thoroughly incorporated. Stir in the brandy. In a separate bowl, sift the flour with the baking soda, baking powder, cinnamon, ginger, nutmeg, cloves, and salt. Stir into the wet ingredients. Fold in the walnuts.

Pour the batter into the prepared pan. Bake for 1 hour, until a toothpick inserted in the center comes out clean. Cool completely on a wire rack before removing from the pan.

{ 5 }

COMING OF AGE

After the events of the late 1960s, the hippies, seekers, and back-to-the-land folk descended on Big Sur. The laid-back and independent community did what it does so well: provide a haven for people during uncertain times. Nepenthe became an essential stop for those on their way to wherever they were going; the restaurant defined itself by throwing open its doors. Where else could someone find a helping hand—including a couch to sleep on, communal dining, and a job—with no questions asked?

1970 marked Nepenthe's twenty-first year; by then it was well on its way but continuing to experience growing pains. My grandfather brought in various people to run the restaurant, "ending in disaster every time," said my aunt Holly. No one could believe the lack of overall systems or accountability that prevailed. The nightly deposits, for example, were placed under my grandmother's pillow in her living room at the end of the night. It wasn't until years later that they bought a safe after the deposit and company truck were stolen on the same night. (When my aunt told my grandfather, he said, "See who doesn't show up for work, and that's who did it.") It was a challenging period with the business in a state of flux, shifting management styles, and ongoing financial concerns.

Herb Evans, who managed the restaurant for a year around that time, recalled trying to balance labor cost with the needs of the staff. "I didn't understand the responsibility" of caring for them, he said. "Lolly thought of them as family; I thought of them as employees." Running Nepenthe was never "business as usual," and what might have worked elsewhere didn't necessarily apply here. "This was the only game in town," he said. "You had to think twice about firing people. This was their livelihood."

Though historically change has been hard to institute at Nepenthe, Herb is credited for having two of the best ideas and one of the worst. The worst was premaking burgers and keeping them under a warmer. He is still teased about that one. However, his natural Vegetarian Chef Salad with seeds and sprouts ushered us into a new age. And his Nepenthe Cheeseboard, with its generous hunks of cheese, fat slices of dark black bread, and fruit served on a board and accompanied by a glass of port was a showstopper. The minute a waiter carried it out to a table, surrounding tables asked for it, too. Both items were '70s versions of California cuisine, and they stayed on the menu for more than twenty years.

Aware that my grandfather hired Herb with the prospect of selling the restaurant to him (Herb had the rock bands Three Dog Night, Black Oak Arkansas, and the Smothers Brothers lined up as potential backers), my grandmother affirmed her own position and told him, "It's good that you're here in one way, but it's not for sale and it never will be." As Herb put it, my grandfather was a gambler and played the market, always having his antennae out, but "it was Lolly's vision that was the strength behind the views and everything."

꒰꒱

My aunt Holly had took over the management of Nepenthe in the mid-'70s. To help her, my grandfather hired Michael Green, our former and current accountant. Under their direction, the corporation became viable, and the Phoenix Shop, struggling financially, was put on its way to profitability. My grandfather was elated, but my grandmother was sometimes more guarded about its direction.

All the same, she never gave up being the face of the business and continued to oversee all that went on there, watching the changing scene from her roost above the restaurant. Throughout most of the '70s she maintained her evening walk through the dining room.

Attitude! Is so important that if not good you will get a nice little vacation . . .
Also, talk about tips and customers on the floor will be noted
and related to me—if you learn to appreciate your opportunity
to serve people you will have little to grumble about.

—NOTE TO THE WAITERS FROM LOLLY, MID-'70S

MAKES 1 LARGE SALAD, SERVING 1 OR 2

4 large handfuls torn salad greens, such as romaine
  and green leaf, washed and crisped
¼ cup sunflower seeds
½ cup cubed medium-sharp Cheddar and Swiss cheese
½ cup chopped carrots
¼ cup sliced black olives
1 hard-cooked egg, peeled and halved
Pinch paprika (optional)
4 thick wedges ripe tomato
About ⅓ cup Roquefort Dressing (page 72) or favorite vinaigrette
Alfalfa sprouts

Vegetarian Chef Salad

Perhaps Nepenthe's greatest selling menu item outside the Ambrosia Burger was the chef salad. With a "Mohawk of sprouts," as someone once described the mountain of alfalfa sprouts on top, and otherwise chock-full of natural goodies, the generous salad evoked that kind of California hippie, health-food lifestyle that others only dreamed about: surfers, sunshine, Volkswagen buses, freedom, and natural living.

The amounts listed are somewhat give or take; administer with abandon and feel free to substitute. Add avocado as some guests used to do. Top with our Roquefort Dressing or your favorite vinaigrette.

Fill a large plate or smaller oval platter with the salad greens. Top with the sunflower seeds, cheese, carrots, and olives. Place the egg halves on either end and dust with a little paprika. Arrange the tomato wedges next to the egg halves. Ladle the dressing over the salad, then top off with a healthy amount of sprouts.

Nepenthe Cheeseboard

Served on a special handle board, the cheeseboard was a showstopper: three kinds of semihard cheeses with an elaborate display of German black bread splayed open, an apple wedged in between, a cluster of grapes spilling over, and a slice of fresh melon tucked underneath.

During the summer months, the restaurant pantry cook could hardly keep up with the demand for the cheeseboard, even though at that time we did not serve fancy cheese, or even great cheese, but good-quality common cheese: aged Tillamook Cheddar, hot pepper Jack, and Monterey Jack, each cut into a thick wedge or block. It wasn't elaborate food, but the presentation and substance knocked people over.

Years later, when I catered weddings and events at the café, I drew on that memory, and always made a gorgeous spread of cheese, fruit, and bread, with the addition of fresh walnuts or almonds, and perhaps a fruit compote (such as Wine-Poached Quince with Rosemary, page 174) or chutney of some kind.

To make your own Nepenthe Cheeseboard, include a crisp apple, a ripe pear, or some other kind of hard fruit that goes well with cheese. Slices of ripe melon or a cluster of grapes are always good, or substitute dried fruit. Think about the color combinations and what kinds of fruits will look and taste good together. Plump cherries, fleshy green or black figs, and small prune plums are nice additions, as are juicy clementines and other citrus fruits in winter. If I was making this today, I might look for locally made cheese, like one of the California Cheddars or a goat's milk Gouda; peppered sheep's milk for the spicy cheese; and for the Jack, a milder creamy cheese, like Cowgirl Creamery's Mt. Tam or Humboldt Fog, a divine ripened goat cheese layered with ash. Even a harder, nutty cheese like St. George, made on the north coast of California, would be a great addition.

Arrange the cheese on a board with the fruit, some of it sliced. Serve with thick slices of hearty German rye or pumpernickel. Cheese, especially artisan quality, is better at room temperature, so let it sit out a bit before serving. Finally, set out a good knife for cutting.

Nepenthe in the 1970s was a richly textured and highly unorthodox place in which to grow up. Some employees and their families lived in their trucks and makeshift trailer homes on and off the property, some found shared housing arrangements or later built original homes on ridgetops, now worth millions. Others lived in the row of rooms along the back parking lot, originally built for the Fassett children. One woman managed to get her baby grand in a pint-size corner room and slept underneath it. Or they lived in the assorted cabins tucked around the property.

We were a way station. An endless stream of curious situations and unusual people came and went. Transients slept on the long benches in the family dining room or camped out on the side of the road near where the school bus arrived. Once a party of guests who found the road closed to the south returned to sleep on my grandmother's living room floor. One very troubled transvestite slept in the bushes near the highway for a short period; I would bring her food in the afternoons after school.

My father, Richard Steele, was one of those who appeared one day back in the early 1960s. An artist and independent thinker, he was thirteen years older than my mother when they met, and involved in the far-out art and beat scene in San Francisco's North Beach and Haight-Asbury before he came to Big Sur. He left soon after I was born, but then returned to live at Nepenthe when I was thirteen years old. Around the same time, I moved away with my mom and siblings. At first, my dad lived in the corrugated-tin shed in the lower garden and worked for my grandmother, collecting the kitchen compost, recycling the coffee grounds, and planting in the garden. While Big Sur and Nepenthe advanced into the new age, he relished the simpler life, saying, "I'll stay a beatnik gardener and carpenter."

He married Elena Salsedo, a French native who worked briefly at Nepenthe chopping lettuce in the late 1970s, and they lived on the property in a little house behind the maintenance shed. Elena was the pastry chef at Ventana Inn for fourteen years. She and my father were a big part of my grandmother's inner circle, sharing weekly dinners with her and her friends.

Among the mix at Nepenthe was a resident bard who recited verse to my grandmother almost nightly; a draftsman who lived in a revamped, purple delivery van equipped with drafting table and bed and who gave me drawing lessons and worked as a gate guard; a whimsical artist with a stained-glass studio in the bottom of the

Phoenix Shop; Geangy, an eccentric seamstress and fortune teller who sewed costumes for the Phoenix boutique and was a caregiver to my grandmother at various times throughout her later life; and a contemporary jeweler who worked out of a studio on the property, eventually becoming nationally known, and who shared weekly Sunday dinners with my grandmother.

Others who appeared at Nepenthe included Robot, a burly character and former Hollywood stuntman who balanced things in the crook of his chin and on his nose—things such as chairs (sometimes with people in them), knives, and even a half-round table. However strange and alarming, he captivated us. Some men became our second uncles, their girlfriends our aunties and companions, and some went on to success. One person who worked there in the 1960s later founded a reputable mountaineering company, and another worked in the music industry in Los Angeles, where his daughter is now a famous actress.

We have also tried to 'let happen' a place where people could be, get their individual lives together and, with luck, learn to work and live together comfortably," my grandmother wrote in a memo to residents. She went on to emphasize her belief in Nepenthe as a symbol of immortality and as a place to be of "love and service" to others. "However imperfect our achievement, it is our purpose to radiate the principles of love and express them through service."

Captivated by unusual and colorful characters, my grandmother made room for those who needed a place to call home. She invited staff and extended family, sometimes up to forty people, into her living room nightly to watch TV. A son of one of the waitresses spent five nights a week there with my grandmother while his mother worked. As was her family kitchen, her living room was a gathering place and sanctuary for many. She remained committed to her community, large and small. It was an ideal she strived for throughout her lifetime, admirable but with its own set of problems and complications, and a model that amused as well as frustrated my grandfather, though he, too, endeavored for that inimitable positioning in the world. Perhaps he even admired her dogged resolve. Nonetheless, her guiding principles required a great deal of patience and understanding by all.

I thought of my mother as a master builder, or an architect. My mother was a woman of action. She loved to develop the talents of people; she wanted to provide the opportunity for them to sing, to paint and to dance.

—GRIFF

Cream Cheese, Walnut, and Raisin Sandwich

This was a classic sandwich served at Nepenthe for years; it is very much reminiscent of my grandmother and the bohemian feel of the place. Filled with cream cheese, lots of nuts and raisins, and sometimes dates; served three halves in a round basket, with a choice of salad; and accompanied by a thick stalk of endive, it inevitably elicited craned necks and raised eyebrows by neighboring tables. "What is that divine-looking sandwich you are eating?" they'd ask. Well, I warn you this is not a sandwich for the uninitiated or for anyone fearing a few calories, but over the years it has had its following, and more recently it received swoons from the restaurant staff when I made it.

Take three slices of good, dark black bread; spread each with a thick layer of cream cheese, softened just a bit, and add a handful each of whole walnuts, sliced black olives, and raisins. If you like, add some chopped dates into the mix as well. Slice each piece in half crosswise, and very carefully press the halves together, tucking in any stray goodies that fall out. Make it for a casual lunch at home, as easy picnic fare, or for teatime, cutting the sandwiches into smaller triangles and passing with napkins.

At Home on the Lower Property

By the early '70s, my mother had married and given birth to my sister Josie. We moved to the lower property, above the canyon, into a small, rustic one-room house with a covered porch. I had a little space off the porch and my brother lived in the loft, and later we added on a room and then another. Our bathroom was a little shack outdoors, frequented by harmless snakes and a frog that lived in the shower. Within a few short years my mother had two more darling little girls, Leah, born at home, and the youngest, Sara, so eventually there were five of us.

There was a large vegetable garden below our house, a sprawling hillside space with rock walls, an orchard with apple, lemon, and orange trees, and one giant avocado tree. A pony named Sheba lived in the corral, and there was a stint of keeping bees. The canyon just beyond, dark and mysterious, was our favorite place to explore, with tall redwood trees, some hollowed out from long ago fires, and a meandering stream that lead to Nepenthe Beach.

Nani, Josie, and Cap

My brother, Cap, had more than seven lives, it seems, having survived being run over by a car backing down the driveway and various other close brushes with moving things. With my three cousins from Sycamore Canyon and the other kids and cousins who frequently visited, we ran all over the property, sometimes playing hide and seek in the Phoenix Shop. We liked to shamelessly break the candy sticks there, so they couldn't be sold but instead given to us.

Cap got his arm stuck in the old-fashioned ring dryer once, the same dryer my aunt Holly got her hair stuck in when she was a girl. By the time my brother was ten years old, he frequently hijacked my mother's Volkswagen Squareback and drove it up and down the road, to and from the restaurant parking lot. After our neighbor gave him a rinky-dink moped, he once tied a rope around one of the beehives and dragged it along behind him up to the family cabin. Of course the bees went after him, later swarming the restaurant's terrace. On the roof of the Phoenix before it became a café, we used to climb out and over the edge onto the railing (a 30 foot drop or more), a devilish act that seems absolutely harrowing now, and one reason the benches along the edge were finally removed.

Ronnie Rugato, a fellow who built us go-carts, used to take all of us kids to the movies in the back of "Brownie," the Nepenthe pickup truck, as did longtime employee and family friend Steve Copeland. We piled in the back with blankets and thick sweaters, singing and shouting all the way to town, then fell fast asleep under the stars on the way home.

MAKES 2 LOAVES

½ cup uncooked wheat berries, soaked overnight
1⅔ cups milk
2 tablespoons butter
⅓ cup honey
1 tablespoon dry yeast
¼ cup lukewarm water
5½ to 6½ cups whole wheat flour
½ cup wheat germ
2 teaspoons salt
1 cup raisins
¼ cup plus 2 tablespoons sunflower seeds
½ cup walnuts, coarsely chopped

Holly's Honey Wheat Berry Bread

My aunt has made this bread ever since I was young. On Christmas, she makes small loaves of it to give as gifts—the recipe can successfully be doubled or tripled. She sometimes adds dried apricots to the mix, and other seeds or nuts. We love it toasted and topped with butter, or better yet, peanut butter and homemade jam.

Simmer the soaked wheat berries in 2 cups water for one hour, until soft. Drain and set aside. Scald the milk, add the butter and honey, and cool to room temperature.

In a large mixing bowl, dissolve the yeast in ¼ cup of lukewarm water. Add the cooled milk mixture, 5½ cups of the flour, wheat germ, and salt; mix well to combine. Add in the wheat berries, raisins, ¼ cup of the sunflower seeds, and walnuts, working in with your hands.

Turn the dough out onto a lightly floured surface; knead until smooth and elastic, adding up to one cup more flour, a little at a time, to prevent the dough from sticking. Place the dough in a clean, lightly oiled bowl, cover, and let rise in a warm place for 1½ to 2 hours, or until it doubles in size.

Preheat the oven to 375°F. Punch down the dough and form into 2 loaves; place the loaves in lightly greased pans. Cover and let rise 45 minutes, or until they double in size. Before baking, brush the top of each loaf with a little water and sprinkle with the remaining sunflower seeds. Bake for 45 to 50 minutes, until golden. Cool the loaves in the pans for 15 minutes, then remove and cool completely on a wire rack.

SERVES 4 TO 6

1 small white onion or 2 large shallots, finely chopped
2 cloves garlic, finely chopped
2 tablespoons olive oil
1½ to 2 cups dry white wine (about half a bottle)
2 small plum tomatoes, chopped (optional)
3 pounds fresh mussels, scrubbed and beards removed
2 tablespoons cold butter
Salt and freshly ground black pepper
3 sprigs fresh parsley or a few basil leaves, finely chopped

Big Sur Mussels, Family Style

Gathering fresh mussels has always been a favorite winter activity in Big Sur and a fun outing with kids. My stepmother, Elena, remembered how one year, during an extended road closure, she and others made Moules Mariniere in the family kitchen for a crowd. This is my version of that French coastal favorite.

Serve the mussels right out of the pot, setting it at the center of the table for all to dig in, as we used to do, or transfer to a warm family-sized bowl for a prettier presentation. Serve with a large green salad and some crusty bread for sopping up the juices.

Sauté the onions and garlic in the oil in a heavy, wide pot over medium heat until soft and translucent. Add the wine and tomatoes and boil for 2 minutes. Add the mussels, cover, and cook, stirring occasionally, until the shells open, 5 to 6 minutes. (Discard any that don't open after 8 to 10 minutes or so.) Transfer the mussels to a warm bowl with a slotted spoon.

Return the broth to high heat. Whisk the butter into the broth and simmer for 2 minutes. Season with salt and pepper. Pour the broth over the mussels and sprinkle with the parsley. Set in the center of the table and pass smaller bowls to your guests.

NOTE: On the California coast you can gather mussels from November through April, but check your local agency before venturing out. Some areas require a permit. Bring an old bucket and a screwdriver or chisel for prying them off the rocks, being careful not to cut your fingers. Fill the bucket partway with seawater for the ride home. Before cooking, scrub the mussels clean and pull off the wispy beards. Discard any that don't open after cooking.

SERVES 4

4 baking apples, such as Gala or Granny Smith
¼ cup golden raisins, plumped in hot water or heated rum
⅓ cup firmly packed brown sugar
¼ cup coarsely chopped pecans
1 teaspoon cinnamon
½ teaspoon nutmeg
2½ tablespoons butter, melted
¼ cup rum or brandy
⅓ cup heavy cream

Baked Cinnamon-Pecan Apples with Rum

These homey, cinnamon-scented baked apples are a classic from my childhood, as close as you can get to an apple pie without actually making one, and nearly as good. You can substitute apple juice or cider for the rum. Serve warm with the thickened cream or with crème fraîche.

Preheat the oven to 375°F.

Core the apples using a sharp pairing knife or melon baller, scooping out some of the flesh, but leaving the apples whole and intact. Make a slit around the middle of each apple to prevent them from exploding while baking.

Combine the raisins, sugar, pecans, cinnamon, and nutmeg in a small bowl. Stir in 2 tablespoons of the melted butter. Drizzle the remaining butter in a small baking dish. Place the apples in the dish. Stuff the hollows with the sugar mixture, packing densely (some of the sugar bits will fall into the pan, which is fine). Pour the rum over the apples.

Cover the dish tightly with aluminum foil. Bake for 30 minutes. Remove the foil and spoon some of the pan juices over the apples. Bake, uncovered, until the apples are cooked through, about 30 minutes longer. Whisk the cream with a fork until lightly thickened, drizzle over the apples, and serve.

Nepenthe is a beautiful place, a haven where public and employees alike live for a timeless moment in Beauty. Lolly's idea, of course, and I have tried to make it viable.

—BILL

A DESTINY OF ITS OWN

By the late 1970s, Big Sur experienced an explosion of visitors. Travel along the two-lane highway had doubled in the previous six years. Going further back, in 1962 only 2,500 cars passed through on an average summer day; by the '70s, closer to 1.4 million motorists traversed the ribboned coastline seasonally.

It was great for business, but there was also much concern over how to deal with the onslaught of visitors and their impact on the environment and the community at large. Photographer Ansel Adams advocated turning Big Sur into a national park, like Yosemite. Architect Nathaniel Owings rallied for his 1960s master plan (the first land use plan to protect the Big Sur coast) to stay in effect. My grandfather feared Big Sur would become the playground of the rich, pointing to the recently opened Ventana Inn, which, according to him, cost $3 million to build. Even so, he seemed to have faith, as my grandmother similarly maintained, that Big Sur and Nepenthe had an amazing destiny. "It's bigger than plans," she said. "The spirit of Nepenthe is what most people come here for. We are in the perfect setting and we should be guardians of its timeless quality."

2¼ cups cake flour
1 teaspoon baking soda
1 teaspoon salt
2 cups granulated sugar
1 cup (2 sticks) butter, room temperature
5 eggs, separated
1 teaspoon pure vanilla extract
1 cup buttermilk
2½ cups unsweetened shredded coconut
2 cups pecans, finely chopped (but not meal)
1 recipe Cream Cheese Icing (page 207)

Italian Wedding Cake

This layered coconut pecan cake, a favorite family recipe, has been used for many Big Sur weddings, including my own. It was first made for my mother's wedding in the early 1970s. I made a few changes, using all butter instead of half Crisco, and cake flour instead of all-purpose flour (if you prefer all-purpose, reduce the amount by ¼ cup).

Preheat the oven to 350°F. Lightly butter and flour two 8-inch round cake pans.

Mix the flour, baking soda, and salt in a small bowl. Set aside 2 tablespoons of the sugar for the egg whites. In a large bowl with an electric mixer, beat the remaining sugar and the butter until fluffy. Beat in the egg yolks, one at a time, and then the vanilla, scraping down the side of the bowl as you go. Mix in the flour mixture on low speed. Add the buttermilk until just blended. Mix in 2 cups of the coconut and 1 cup of the pecans.

In a separate very clean bowl, beat the egg whites with the reserved 2 tablespoons sugar until stiff. Whisk a third of the whites into the cake batter, and then fold in the rest.

Divide the batter between the prepared pans, spreading evenly. Bake in the middle rack of the oven for 30 minutes, until a toothpick inserted in the middle comes out clean. Cool the cakes on a rack for 10 minutes. Run a knife around the cake edges to loosen, and then turn out onto a rack. Cool completely.

Place one layer on a cake plate. Spread with the icing and scatter the remaining coconut and pecans over the top. Top with the second layer. Spread the remaining icing over the top and side.

Kim on her wedding day

THE JUICE BAR, CAFÉ AMPHORA

In the early to mid-'70s my grandmother turned the little guard shack on the Phoenix roof terrace into a seasonal place called the Juice Bar. It went through various incarnations in the first few years, including one as a hot dog stand. The first year my stepfather ran it, he served only two sandwiches; a natural salad layered with nuts, raisins, and chopped raw vegetables; and two desserts. My mother made her carrot cake, a hearty, earthy loaf with cream cheese frosting, and brownies from a recipe off the back of a Ghirardelli can. Another season there were Latin-flavored pita-bread pizzas, smeared with beans, tomatoes, slices of avocado, and salsa. I have fond memories of one of the later incarnations, sitting at the counter as a budding teenager, eating plump strawberries sprinkled with sugar and fresh cream poured over the top.

In the late '70s, Domenico Vastarella, an animated Italian from Naples who fit right into my grandmother's milieu, took over, installing a couple of toaster ovens and serving strong coffee and baked eggs with a sprinkling of herbs. By his second season they had renamed it Café Amphora and had a large honey-colored amphora (vessel) sent over from Italy to mark the entrance. Domenico updated the food to include more Eurocentric fare. My grandmother's artist friend Edmund Kara sculpted the redwood turtle fountain. There was a grand unveiling under its new name, all very fitting for the time and place and how my grandmother imagined it.

The late Bob Wilson (pictured), former owner of what was then Carmel Café, and his wife, Robin, took over in 1980 and created the Café Amphora that is most remembered today. Robin made all the baked goods in a tiny, tiny triangular kitchen with one shared oven and barely enough room to sneeze. Revered for its brunch, including perfectly cooked eggs Benedict and homemade pies, it had a laid-back, colorful atmosphere and became a well-loved local hangout and a preferred setting for weddings in the spirit and style of Big Sur country.

The Wilsons nurtured the setting, planting flowers and trailing vines on the redwood arbor. They played vibrant world music, giving it an eclectic feel, and served espresso drinks long before the restaurant did. For just over ten years, they ran the place (Robin ran it on her own in the last few years), living on the property with their three children and a dog named Ari. Like others, they shared in my grandmother's Sunday night dinners and were intimately involved in her life. Robin cooked family meals for three seasons in the early 1980s, and Bob was instrumental in staging holiday dinners alongside my grandmother for many years.

SERVES 4

HOLLANDAISE SAUCE
3 egg yolks
2 tablespoons fresh lemon juice
¾ cup (1½ sticks) butter, melted and solids skimmed off
Pinch salt and a pinch white pepper
Tabasco or Sriracha hot sauce

EGGS, MUFFINS, AND TOPPINGS
8 eggs, chilled
4 multigrain English muffins, split
8 slices Canadian bacon, pan grilled
1 avocado, halved, pitted, peeled, and sliced into thin wedges
Chopped fresh parsley, for garnish

Café Benedict

Café Amphora became known for its perfectly cooked eggs Benedict on grain muffins in the 1980s, and Café Kevah is now known for it as well. With the magnificent view and outdoor seating, there is no better place to enjoy this decadent breakfast classic. You can add a variety of toppings, like avocado and ham, as shown, or lightly steamed crab. For a brunch setting, set out a platter of options and let your guests choose.

For the Hollandaise sauce, whisk the yolks with 1 teaspoon of water in a bowl set over simmering water for about 2 minutes, until pale yellow and a ribbon forms when running the back of a spoon through the surface. Be careful not to scramble the eggs. Whisk in the lemon juice. Turn off the heat but leave the bowl over the warm pot. Slowly whisk in the butter in a steady stream, then whisk vigorously for 30 seconds or so to thoroughly combine. Add the salt, pepper, and Tabasco to taste. Move the pot to the back of the stove while preparing the eggs.

For the eggs, have a medium pot of water simmering at a rapid speed. One at a time, crack the eggs into a small bowl and then gently slip them into the simmering water. Cook 2 minutes for soft yolks, or longer if you like them harder.

Meanwhile, toast the muffins and arrange 2 on each plate. Top with the bacon and avocado.

Scoop out the poached eggs with a slotted spoon and gently rest on a towel for just a second to soak up any water. Nestle one egg onto each muffin, and top with Hollandaise sauce. Sprinkle parsley over the tops.

MAKES 1 (9-INCH) PIE, SERVING 8

½ recipe Holly's Pie Dough (page 292), made with all butter

¼ cup (½ stick) butter, room temperature
¾ cup firmly packed brown sugar
¼ cup granulated sugar
4 eggs
¾ cup Lyle's Golden Syrup or barley malt syrup
1 tablespoon flour
1 teaspoon pure vanilla extract
2 cups whole walnuts

Amphora Walnut Pie

Delectably gooey and sticky sweet, this favorite pie from Café Amphora is a keeper.

Preheat the oven to 350°F. Roll out the pie dough and fit into a 9-inch pie pan. Flute the edges and chill until ready to use.

Using an electric mixer, beat the butter with the brown sugar and granulated sugar until light and fluffy. Beat in the eggs one at a time, scraping down the bowl after each addition, until incorporated. Beat in the syrup, flour, and vanilla.

Fold in the walnuts. Pour the filling into the pie shell. Bake for 1 hour, until a knife inserted in the middle comes out clean. The pie will puff up and can become quite brown. Cover with aluminum foil to prevent the top from burning if necessary.

CARROT CAKE
1 cup unbleached white flour
1 cup whole-wheat flour
2 teaspoons cinnamon
2 teaspoons baking powder
1 teaspoon baking soda
½ teaspoon salt
1 cup canola oil
¾ cup granulated sugar
¾ cup firmly packed brown sugar
4 eggs
2 cups grated carrots (about 3 large carrots)
1 cup crushed pineapple, with juice
1 cup chopped walnuts or pecans
1 cup raisins

CREAM CHEESE ICING
8 ounces cream cheese, room temperature
½ cup (1 stick) butter, room temperature
2 cups confectioners' sugar, sifted
1 teaspoon pure vanilla extract

Kim's Loaf Carrot Cake

My mother made these cakes for the Juice Bar, baking them in loaf pans and selling thick slices right out of the pans. It is a family favorite.

Preheat the oven to 350°F. Line the bottom of 2 loaf pans with parchment paper, then lightly butter and dust with flour.

For the cake, sift together the white flour, whole-wheat flour, cinnamon, baking powder, baking soda, and salt. Mix the oil with the granulated sugar and brown sugar in a large bowl. Stir in the eggs, mixing well after each, then add the carrots and pineapple. Add the dry ingredients and stir to combine. Fold in the nuts and raisins.

Divide the batter between the prepared pans. Bake for 35 to 40 minutes, until a toothpick inserted into the centers comes out clean. Cool on wire racks for 15 minutes. Remove from the pans and cool completely before frosting.

For the icing, beat the cream cheese and butter in a medium bowl until light and fluffy. Add the confectioners' sugar and beat until smooth. Stir in the vanilla.

Spread the icing over the tops and sides of each cake.

Sign Parties

Astrology parties, or sign parties as they became known, were monthly events occurring on the last Wednesday of each zodiac sign. Started as a way to celebrate employees' birthdays back in the 1960s (or earlier), they expanded to include anyone having a birthday that month and featured complimentary cake and Champagne. Essentially they became community-wide birthday bashes and a magnet for young people who flocked to them to dance under the stars.

The parties began at 9:00 p.m. with a mass birthday sing-along to Stevie Wonder's "Happy Birthday." Everyone who was celebrating a birthday sat around a large round table filled with homemade cakes, one at each place. It was a grand mosaic of cake display, a smattering of pattern, color, and shape with every flavor imaginable. Birthday celebrants blew out the candles and feverishly cut and passed cake, a multitude of hands reaching for a slice or two. On my twenty-first birthday, my aunt Holly made a special cake just for me, a light, meringue-like confection filled with custard and berries, and I sat in front of it and beamed.

When I was younger, the kids weren't allowed to be on the terrace once the party began, unless it was a child's birthday, and if so, only for a short time. I watched the sign parties with my cousins and siblings from my grandmother's window in the log cabin just above the terrace. We stretched out on her chenille-covered beds, four of them running the length of the cabin wall in an L shape, chins perched in hands, and watched the endless dancing that went on below.

3 cups cake flour, or 2½ cups plus
    2 tablespoons unbleached white flour
2 teaspoons baking powder
¾ teaspoon salt
1 cup (2 sticks) butter, room temperature
1½ cups granulated sugar
4 eggs, separated
2 teaspoons pure vanilla extract
⅔ cups milk

My Favorite Birthday Cake

This is a versatile cake, a recipe I've made for my daughter Nicoya's birthday every year since she was very young. It is based on a simple butter cake we made for Nepenthe's astrology parties. Fill it with fresh fruit, or jam and top with whipped cream as in the variation below, or simply dust with confectioners' sugar. You can also flavor the cake with orange or lemon zest or the seeds of a vanilla bean, or make it plain.

Preheat the oven to 350°F. Lightly butter and flour two 8- or 9-inch round cake pans.

Sift the flour with the baking powder and salt in a medium bowl. In a large bowl, beat the butter with a wooden spoon or electric mixer until light and creamy. Add the sugar and beat until fluffy, scraping down the side, about 5 minutes. Beat in the egg yolks one at a time, mixing well after each. Stir in the vanilla. Alternately stir in the flour mixture and the milk a little at a time, mixing well to combine.

Beat the egg whites in a clean metal bowl until they hold a soft peak. Whisk one-third of the egg whites into the batter. Fold in the remaining whites, stirring gently until just incorporated.

Divide the batter between the prepared pans. Bake for 30 to 35 minutes, until a toothpick inserted in the centers comes out clean. Cool on a rack.

Variation: To make the jam cake (pictured), place one cake layer on a platter or large plate. Spread with 1 cup Simple Blackberry Jam (page 263) or other preserves. Whip 1 cup heavy cream with 3 or more tablespoons sugar until soft peaks form. Whisk in 1 teaspoon pure vanilla extract. Spread whipped cream on top of the cake, serving any extra on the side. Garnish with fresh berries.

Lolly by Jane Powers, 1930s

FIN DE SIÈCLE

My grandmother died suddenly on January 19, 1986, shocking family and friends and throwing the restaurant into a flurry of unrest. She was seventy-four years old and had undetected cancer, but died of a heart attack in the hospital. It was as if a dam broke and there was no stopping the flood of people who arrived for days to gather in her living room, share stories, wander through her garden, and spend time in the reminders of her immense life. Letters sending love from around the world poured in, from senators, congressmen, artists, and authors. The love and widespread feeling of loss was palpable.

More than 300 friends and family came to pay tribute at her memorial. They ate Ambrosia Burgers and sipped sangria (page 216) while sitting on the terrace, and all day they paraded up to her private garden where her ashes rested in a shiny brass tea kettle before being buried there. The shininess of the urn gave everyone a good laugh, as she would have wanted it with a patina.

My grandfather moderated what he called a love feast in "Jerry Lewis style," according to a newspaper. Between a roller coaster of tears and laughter, he regaled our family, employees, and the masses with his stories about my grandmother—his wife of more than fifty years (they never divorced)—and Nepenthe's history.

He told the story of jumping ship in Oregon while a merchant marine and hitching a ride to see her in San Francisco. "When should we get married?" he asked her straight off. "Yesterday," she replied, and soon after they did.

He told another story of coming home one day and telling her he'd lost his $65-per-month job, and she said, "That's too bad, because I'm pregnant again." Everyone laughed. "But what will I do?" he cried, and she assured him that "you'll make it, and you'll be proud some day."

"I *am* proud," he said looking out at all of us gathered around. "I have a beautiful family, five children [with her], fourteen grandchildren, and one great-grandchild, and she loved them all."

Between my grandfather's reveling, old friends and people we didn't even know got up and told stories. Frank Trotter, who built the restaurant with his brother Walter (the two were pillars of the Big Sur community), remarked how she worked as hard as any of them on building it, remembering how my grandfather still had time to read the paper and listen to the radio, while she would be out there hauling rocks and pouring concrete. "She did more for the Big Sur community than anyone I know," he said. Others told of visiting when Nepenthe was in its infancy, the lazy afternoons that drifted into night, the playing poker or dominoes into the wee hours of the morning. They recalled her generosity and kindheartedness, her Sunday night dinners, her family kitchen, her sympathy cards during times of loss, her loans of money, the job she gave them when they couldn't get one anywhere else, the clothes, food, and sometimes a bed to lay their heads that she provided.

My aunt Holly remembered a string of stories about the oddball characters my grandmother took in and cared for. One man, a wandering poet who worked for us and lived on and off the property for many years, got up and said quietly, "I was one of them," and then he cried. My grandfather later read a poem for Lolly from another wandering bard, with a line that asked the question, "Who's going to give Bibles to the children now that she is gone?"

The feeling that day was surreal, moody, lethargic, almost delayed in its reaction, like the morning after a storm when it is strangely calm and yet everything is a wreck and feels so uncertain and fragile. People were walking around in a daze and in disbelief, with so many questions and concerns, and my grandmother, usually there to offer measured composure to people's fears and worry, was there no longer. Lolly had been the anchor not only to her children and all her grandchildren, but to so many others as well, her community spread around the world, more than we even knew.

The ceremony itself brimmed with my grandmother's creative spirit, opening with a passing of bread, a beautiful ringed loaf made by Barbara Woyt "as a symbol of our togetherness with Mom," said Holly. A woman played "Amazing Grace" on a bamboo flute, accompanied by a pianist, and everyone sang along. Some were wearing costumes and clothing she had made. My mother wrapped herself in one of my grandmother's woolen shawls. Douglas Madsen spoke of the magical week they spent together on the island of Capri when they were both so young, and how much he would miss her. Former state senator and environmentalist Fred Farr told about getting his car stuck in a ditch in the middle of the night, and by the time he got it out, around 2:00 a.m., "there was Lolly with a beautiful meal for us."

The actor Jack Lambert (a tough guy in many old Westerns), a longtime friend whom my mother said used to come and sleep by the fire in the living room in the early days and who adored my grandmother, recalled the magical life she created on top of the hill. He recited the R. Lee Sharpe poem, "A Bag of Tools," and raised the roof to her remarkable spirit. "Our Lolly made so many stepping-stones, for so many."

Lolly was Nepenthe. Lolly treated everyone the same. We were all hungry and homeless. Whether rich or poor, crazy or sane, famous or not, if she could, she would lend a helping hand, give us a job, a place to live, food to eat, something to wear, or simple friendship with no motive on her part. I can still feel her spirit on the property, and her memory will always live in my heart.

—STEVE BOWERS, FORMER BAR MANAGER

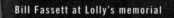
Bill Fassett at Lolly's memorial

1 orange
1 lime
1 lemon
⅓ cup granulated sugar
1 (750-milliter) bottle fruity Spanish red wine
1 (750-milliter) bottle Spanish rosé
Seltzer water or 7UP

Sangria à la Nepenthe

It didn't get much better than sitting on the terrace bleachers with friends, whiling away a perfectly good afternoon over a pitcher of Nepenthe's fruit-laced sangria. Certainly the view and the people watching added to its mystique, making a glass à la Nepenthe that much more memorable. Or could it be, also, that the sangria was steeped, usually overnight? Old-timers remember big buckets of the fruity celebration drink sloshing around in the back, slowly fermenting, like a fine wine, giving that final glass a just-right touch of age.

Slice the orange, lime, and lemon into ¼-inch-thick rounds. Place half of each in a large bucket or glass jar. Halve each of the remaining slices, cover with plastic, and refrigerate to use later as garnish. Sprinkle the fruit in the jar with the sugar. Using a muddle or the back of a wooden spoon, muddle the fruit so that it releases its juice. Pour in the wine and rosé and stir for a minute or so, until the sugar dissolves. Set aside, loosely covered and at room temperature, to steep for at least 30 minutes, or longer for better flavor.

Chill the sangria before serving. Transfer to a glass pitcher. Pour into fluted glasses filled with ice and top each with a splash of seltzer or 7UP. Garnish with reserved slices of fruit.

I have given my life to Nepenthe because I believe in the essence of the way of life here—inside and outside. Don't underestimate these values—it may not sound businesslike but it is the truth.

— LOLLY

My grandmother's death clearly symbolized a changing of the guard, if not on paper (managers at this time still reported to my grandfather), in practical terms for sure. One friend of hers remarked that Nepenthe changed immediately after her death, a sentiment that I heard time and time again.

In a letter to my grandfather's cousin, Nixon Griffis, on March 16, 1985, less than a year before she died, my grandmother points to the future generation. "Kirsten stepped in and took over for Holly—he is doing a terrific job—and is incorporating some new ideas which are pretty sound as he has grown up around Nepenthe and her many dilemmas . . . It is wonderful for me to watch all the grandchildren and the other youngsters, that grew up here, move into solid positions here at Nepenthe."

Her death devastated those in her inner circle. The family kitchen closed down within days and Sunday dinners ended. Her living room was no longer a place for gathering and was subsequently closed off to old friends. These were changes that were inevitable but also upsetting, and they largely altered the milieu and feeling of the place.

"The question that has perplexed me for years is: 'Is it the place, or is it the people?'" said Stefano Cacace, who dined with my grandmother every Sunday night for fifteen years. "And I've come to the conclusion that it's the people that make the place, because the place is always there, but it's the people that give it that type of life. That is what your grandmother created for all of us, a space that allowed us to feel comfortable enough to maybe think in a different way than we would have normally thought if we were just living in, you know, Pacific Grove. She was always there. She was always there for you."

HOMECOMING

Within months of my grandmother's death, I returned home from Hawaii, where I had been living for two years, and moved into the log cabin. I once again slept in her big bed in the back room as I did as a child, and spent my afternoons curled up on the row of beds in her living room, where the still life of her legacy remained intact. I was twenty years old.

During meetings in the living room with my aunt Holly and her son Kirk we would hash out some detail of her story or talk about what to do with the family kitchen. I remember the warmth of the morning sun hitting the brass lantern above the round table and the Italian glass fishing balls in a tarnished bowl staged at the table's center; I remember the last meals around the family kitchen table and lighting the potbelly stove in the early morning before work. I felt the strange quietness without her there and the solitude of the midnight hour, when she would have turned in to sleep. Within that first year, the family began to unearth the myriad treasures, books, and stacks of papers tucked throughout the cabin and slowly began to distribute the bits and pieces from her life.

A year after moving back I married Mark Hudson, best friend of my cousin Kirk. He grew up in Big Sur, and like many other Big Sur children, spent a great deal of time around Nepenthe, attending parties and family dinners. He worked there as both a teenager and as an adult. Mark's great-grandfather was William G. Hudson, a prominent lawyer who, along with his two law partners, acquired 6,000 acres of land on the south coast, just past Esalen, in the early 1900s. There were no roads then, and they came down on horseback and used it for hunting. In 1991, our son, Trevor, was born there, in a magical room built by Mark's father, on the edge of the hill, with an incredible view of the canyon.

We were married on the terrace of Nepenthe on a bright summer morning just before the restaurant opened, surrounded by employees, family, and friends. Steve Copeland was the master of ceremonies. Tying in with the theatrics of my childhood, I wore an ivory taffeta dress fashioned after flamenco costumes from my grandmother's closet, and a festive multicolored veil. Mark wore a borrowed black tuxedo and a traditional maile lei, sent by friends, around his neck. Two red-tailed hawks circled us, as they did the day my grandmother died and again during her memorial. The stage was set, as my grandmother would have likened it, and so my own family began.

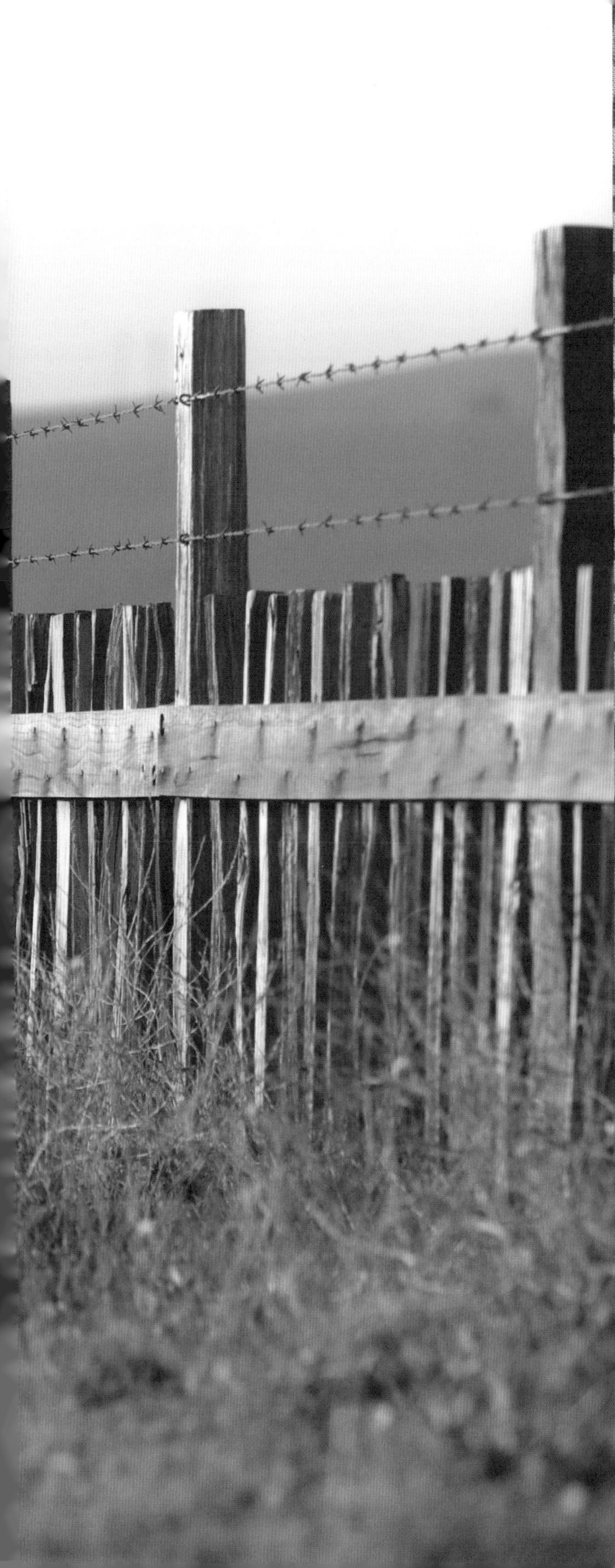

CHAPTER 6

End of an Era

$\mathcal{F}$orget your worldly cares at Nepenthe's gay pavilion.
Where the Phoenix bird repairs and is feeling like a million.

—FROM NEPENTHE'S MENU

{ 6 }

END OF AN ERA

The 1990s brought further change after my grandmother's passing and a resolute shift to the next generation as my grandfather stayed in the background. It was also a time of flourishing, of energy and excitement, as Nepenthe evolved and matured. Many of my generation, now grown, returned to work at the restaurant, some only during summer when out of college, or some, like me, and others who came for the longer term, infusing the restaurant with fresh ideas and a new outlook. Just up the road, the luxurious Post Ranch Inn opened, bringing renewed attention to Big Sur as a top destination and with it new guests who savored our casual atmosphere and legendary views. During this time the family took over the café operation, paving the way for on-site weddings and events under my direction.

The family finally moved into the profession of running a restaurant as opposed to a "happening," remarked Tom Birmingham, manager at the time. While there was less emphasis on the communal approach, a marked but inevitable change from the way my grandmother operated, we kept her legacy of care in mind. Under the combined management of my cousin Kirk Gafill and his mother, Holly Fassett, and with Tom running the restaurant, Nepenthe grew as a business and became more profitable in ways never experienced before.

It was still a transition period, with many shifts in personnel and policy. Many of the staff that worked there for years, and some for decades, left, causing further change after my grandmother's death and upsetting the status quo. Gone were the vague job descriptions and blurred expectations for those living on the property. The days of waitresses in long, flowing skirts, dancing nightly after work, and free drinks for all staff once their shifts were over were long gone, too, as much due to a cultural shift as to changing management styles. Where waiters once made their own colorful aprons and wore them along with small shoulder bags for tips, they now wore uniform commercial aprons purchased by the restaurant. They also had to show up for staff trainings, stop smoking while on the floor, and learn the new computer system.

Cooks no longer called out names like "Helen, please," to let waiters know an order was ready for pickup. Instead, the waitstaff had pagers. (Neither did patrons hear a grouchy shout-out, as could also be the case. Once, years before, after the day cook continued to demand baskets in a droning voice, a man sitting at a nearby table called out, "Can someone please give the poor guy some baskets?")

It didn't lose all its life, though, and there remained a core group of staff with a long history at Nepenthe, including Pasadena Playhouse alum Archie Hess. Jill Bowers, who worked at Nepenthe for more than twenty years, shared a nightly kiss and a glass of wine over the counter with her bartender husband, Steve, at shift's end. They occasionally took a whirl on the dance floor. Joanne (Jojo) Fletcher, longtime waitress and cook, peppered her shifts with humor and optimism, as did waitress Susie Derr. Willie Nelson, who started cooking on the line in the 1960s at age twelve, continued to sling burgers as well as anyone half her age. At the Phoenix Shop, Michele Peterson imbued my grandmother's spirit, bringing an artist's eye and dramatic flair to the clothing boutique, as did then-manager Linda Fisher.

Many of the changes brought renewed focus and a necessary lift to the daily floor show. A burst of fresh talent and creative interest simmered around the property, and in some cases a more willing staff made the changes viable. As one waitress told me, "Nepenthe moved into the times." To her mind, it was not so out of line with what was happening in most restaurants elsewhere. "It just matured into a business."

The lively and sometimes disruptive bar scene quieted down as well, the wilder antics of the night scene a distant past. (Actor Bill Murray once danced on one of the half-round tables with all the waiters during a sign party. As he was leaving, he reportedly told the bartender, "That was the best time I ever had.") "Dirty Corner" had fewer regulars as we became stricter about drinking limits. Our one-time mile-long "86 List" of people not allowed to drink at the bar grew shorter, and there were fewer disturbances overall. But there were still dissenters. A new espresso machine at the bar caused some of the bartenders to threaten to quit as it was seen as too much trouble and too fancy. Even so, Nepenthe remained a place for gathering and having a good time.

I've never seen the moon look more beautiful than it is now, and I've walked on the moon.

—EDWIN "BUZZ" ALDRIN, ASTRONAUT

My grandmother's creative force and artistic heritage imbue Nepenthe to this day. Today there is definition and a clear business model, both sides of the coin as necessary as night and day, a game of balance. Kirk and my aunt Holly work hard to uphold my grandparents' intentions and ideals and strive to maintain that symmetry.

To better the overall experience at the restaurant, my cousin Kirk and manager Tom Birmingham initiated service training and wine education. Tom started what he called "Let's Make a Deal" wine program with emphasis on value wines and a California-wine-by-the-glass list.

With the combined efforts by our cooks and a newly appointed management team, we became more aware of our menu's strengths and weaknesses. We paid more attention to the food, adding vegetarian specials and new desserts as well as a wider selection of fresh fish from a quality, certified purveyor. New relationships with suppliers were a partial benefit of the opening of the Sierra Mar restaurant at the Post Ranch, which in some cases meant better products at a better price.

While our menu didn't change much, the way we executed it improved, and we hired a cook to manage the prep department. It had moved from the unworkable, tight, and colorfully painted restaurant kitchen to the family kitchen, remodeled with the addition of a walk-in refrigerator, two commercial stoves, and a hood. The family table moved over to my aunt Holly's house.

The changes, on occasion, sparked great debate among staff and even family, but, ultimately, the new rules paved the way for tremendous growth and gave staff and family a renewed sense of pride in their working environment. No longer were people just working there to get by or for the love of my grandmother and the community she created. Employees now had a greater stake in the financial success of the restaurant, helped by a 401(k) savings program for full-timers, and with that came new responsibilities and a heightened awareness around job performance.

Nepenthe changed from a happening to a restaurant. That "restaurantness" is still informed by that old, unique history, the legacy of care that Bill and Lolly put into play.

—TOM BIRMINGHAM

The presence of family and extended family remained strong, sometimes with decades-long connections. As Tom once pointed out, there was a time when he used to be able to say to a customer, "In 1925, Sam Trotter built this log cabin, his sons living nearby built the restaurant, one of the daughters (Tootie Trotter) baked that pie, and her daughter just waited on you." Several family members worked and lived on the property at any given time, including my sisters, my cousins, and my mother, Kim, and me, thus continuing my grandparents' dream of keeping Nepenthe as family-run. My cousin Erin lived in the log cabin with her husband, Tom Birmingham, and family, and she still does today. Her daughter Emily was born there. My sister Josie's son Benjamin was also born on the property in the old sewing room, as was my daughter Nicoya, arriving a few years later, in one of the houses overlooking the beach. On the days my grandfather dropped by, all four generations might be present, the youngest at that time being my son Trevor.

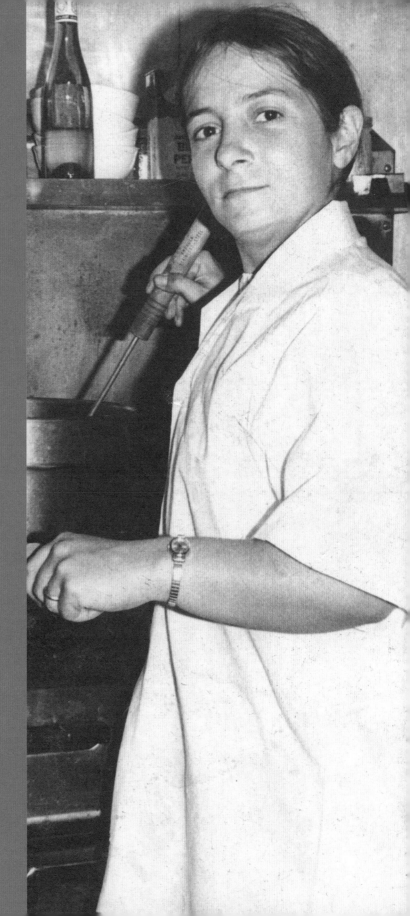

Willie Nelson

The daughter of old-time bartender George Lopes and cook Dotty, who also worked in the office, Willie began working at Nepenthe at the age of twelve. My grandfather hired her and my mother as cooks and salad chefs on the busy weekends. They were barely tall enough to see over the counter, and she remained so.

Early on, she tried her hand as a waitress, showing up to work in a purple polyester pantsuit, but after a few hours, she decided it wasn't for her. As a cook, she once tossed a hamburger on a customer's head after he repeatedly returned it, the last time bringing it up to the counter himself. My grandfather apparently agreed with her youthful tactics and gave her a raise.

Full of laughs and good jokes, Willie still works at Nepenthe almost fifty years later, as vice president of the corporation and in charge of human resources. In the family tradition, Willie's son, Greg Nelson, a childhood friend of mine, bartends at Nepenthe.

DADDY BILL'S LAST YEARS

In the early 1980s, my grandfather lived in a condo in Carmel with my brother, Cap, who was still in high school at that time. As the years passed he became less active. Always a gambler and ever hopeful for the big payoff, he spent a great deal of time at home in his living room, watching the stock market on TV in his pajamas. My grandmother sent him a note the year before she died, encouraging him to take better care of himself and suggesting he get dressed every day. "Please hear me," she wrote. "I love you and am concerned about things getting out of hand."

It is touching to read this, knowing their long history and the difficulties they faced together and apart. It reminds me of when my grandmother and I visited him one afternoon. He sat hunched over in a low-slung chair, while she was across from him. Staying fixated on the numbers going up and down on the screen, he occasionally threw out a funny joke, looking up to see her reaction, and then busting into a broad smile and a deep chuckle. He still made her laugh. She still cared for him.

What do writers write about? They write about Bill Fassett.

—RICHARD de MILLE

Following my grandmother's death, he moved into a Carmel house with Alice Russell and their daughter, Havrah, along with Alice's sister Gina, who took care of him, and son Patrick. It was reassuring to visit him there, a place for all his friends, children, and grandchildren to visit. He was still our anchor, a needed father figure for some of us; many of the kids I grew up with—not only the blood-related ones—looked to Daddy Bill in that way. When we were younger we all took turns staying with him in Carmel. He once took me to meet Clint Eastwood at the tennis club, where he played regularly. Buck Bemis, a friend from the old days, said of my grandfather's game, "If a ball came near him, he was lethal." During the summers, my grandfather took all of us kids to Lake Nacimiento for a week on a flat-roofed houseboat.

In his last years, he still carried on about something he had recently read, his renewed interest in mysticism, and thoughts on politics, baseball, and history. His oldest friends continued to visit and write him letters. Attorney Bill Stewart, one of a group of friends who played poker for more than thirty years and a founder of the original Doc Rickets Lab on Cannery Row, essentially a private "drinking and eating" club that my grandfather frequented in its heyday, recalled the good old days at Nepenthe's bar with my grandfather. He marveled at meeting novelist James Baldwin, whom they later invited to their private club. He especially admired my grandfather's sense of humor. "He was either laughing at you or with you," he recalled warmly.

Going through some of his papers, I was amazed to find correspondence with well-known authors, including Dr. M. Scott Peck, who wrote *The Road Less Traveled*. Richard de Mille, son of the award-winning filmmaker Cecil B. De Mille, sent him chapters of a book in progress about none other than my grandfather himself. "What do writers write about?" he inscribed on the page. "They write about Bill Fassett."

CAFE
KEVAH

IN THE RES... ... UPSTAIRS
AFTER 10:30 am DOWNSTAIR...
IN THE PHOENIX SHOP

CAFÉ KEVAH

In 1992, our family took over the café operation, formerly run for more than ten years by Bob and Robin Wilson as Café Amphora. When it closed in the winter of 1991, as it did every year for the winter season, Nepenthe ended their informal lease. Then, after extensive remodeling and a concept change, it reopened it as Café Kevah the following spring.

Café Kevah became my baby. Besides working at the restaurant (and studying design), I had been catering weddings and select events, using the family-prep kitchen to operate from, and I was ready to branch out when my cousin offered me the café. I was twenty-six years old. I spent months planning, rebuilding the space with our maintenance crew, crafting the concrete tables and countertop and a new lighting system, traveling to San Francisco for inspiration, and creating a new menu and raising three kids (two stepsons Zachariah and Dylan, and nine-month-old Trevor). My mother returned to Nepenthe during this time, after years of being away, and worked closely with me at the café, as did my youngest sister, Sara.

Kirk, Tom, and I took an inaugural planning trip to San Francisco to taste our way through the cafés and restaurants we thought might be inspirational, including the Lark Creek Inn, Stars Restaurant and Bakery, and Campton Place, where we were inspired by the homey breakfast fare, the baskets of flaky pastries, buttery crumb cakes, scones, homemade granola, and preserves. I wrote abundant notes and scribbled drawings of things we liked. We bought books and studied floor plans, takeout counters, the Zuni Café's colored cement tables, how food arrived, and what it came on.

Enthused about simple European food while influenced by our Latino cooks and my love of Mexico's earthy cuisine, we came up with a menu that was experimental and eclectic from the beginning, drawing inspiration from around the map and highlighting local ingredients.

Cheri Gladstone, a chef from the East Coast, helped me plan and create the café's first menu, featuring small plates: grilled meat and fish brochettes topped with a variety of salsas and accompaniments; our breakfasts featured comfort food like Buttermilk French Toast with Apple Pear Butter (page 255) and Café Kevah granola (page 253). We spent weeks making test menus and presenting food ideas on the back porch of Nepenthe's family kitchen to a select group of family and friends. Our opening event featured a mariachi-style band, and we served festive small bites in keeping with our menu. The café was named in honor of my grandfather's mother, Kevah, and he attended in good cheer.

In the beginning, we served brunch all day, but after a while we stopped around noon to accommodate our growing lunch crowd. Today, after further adjusting the menu, the café again serves brunch throughout the day. As business expanded and our experience grew, we moved into catering events when there was little chance of rain, a whole new challenge. A year after the birth of my beautiful daughter Nicoya, I left the café for family reasons. It was a difficult decision and not something I planned for. I later worked at Sierra Mar Restaurant as their pastry chef.

NEPEN
RESTAVI
VPSTA
OPEN FROM

SERVES 4

4 pasilla chiles
6 to 8 ounces Monterey Jack cheese or queso fresco, shredded
6 eggs
1 cup milk
½ cup half-and-half
Dash nutmeg
1 teaspoon salt
Dash white pepper
Salsa Fresca (page 241)
Chopped cilantro, for garnish
Corn tortillas, warmed

Chile Custards with Salsa Fresca

A favorite of our staff and guests when the café first opened, these individual savory custards puff up beautifully in the oven but quickly deflate once removed, so serve immediately. Top with Salsa Fresca and serve with warmed corn tortillas on the side.

Preheat the oven to 375°F.

Place the chiles in a small saucepan, cover with water, and bring to a boil. Boil for 5 to 10 minutes, until soft. Drain and leave unpeeled. When cool enough to handle, make a 2-inch slit on one side in each, starting below the stem and keeping the chile intact. Remove the seeds and stuff with the cheese. Place 1 chile in each of 4 of the 5-inch ramekins and put the ramekins on a small baking sheet.

Whisk the eggs, milk, half-and-half, nutmeg, salt, and pepper until thoroughly combined. Pour over the chiles. They won't be completely covered. Carefully place the baking sheet in the oven and bake until the custard is set and nicely browned, 15 to 20 minutes.

Set each ramekin on a plate, top with a little salsa, and garnish with cilantro. Serve immediately with the tortillas.

SERVES 4

CHICKEN SKEWERS
1 pound boneless skinless chicken breast
2 cloves garlic, finely chopped
¼ bunch fresh cilantro or basil (or both), leaves only, chopped
Salt and freshly ground black pepper
Juice of 1 or 2 limes, to taste
3 or 4 tablespoons olive oil

MANGO SALSA
1 firm but ripe mango, peeled and diced
1 small cucumber, peeled, seeded, and diced
½ red onion, diced
½ bunch fresh cilantro, leaves only, finely chopped
1 lime, halved
Salt and white pepper

SALAD
2 large handfuls field greens or arugula,
    rinsed and crisped in the refrigerator
Olive oil (optional)
Lime wedges, for serving
Corn tortillas, warmed

Cilantro Chicken Skewers with Mango Salsa

The café's signature tapa was skewered chicken or salmon topped with mango-papaya salsa and served on a bed of organic field greens, with corn tortillas on the side.

I now add cucumber to the salsa for a nice crunch and balance of flavor, and occasionally substitute basil for the cilantro or use both. I do not add jalapeño, but you can make a spicier salsa, as the kitchen guys preferred, by adding no more than a ½ jalapeño (seeded and finely minced). Keep in mind a balance of flavor, texture, and color as you prepare the salsa, adjusting accordingly.

For the chicken skewers, slice the chicken breast lengthwise into 1-inch-wide strips. Place in a shallow dish and scatter around the garlic, cilantro, salt, and pepper. Squeeze lime juice over the top and cover with the oil. Marinate for 30 minutes or so, turning the chicken halfway through to coat both sides.

Meanwhile, for the salsa, combine the mango, cucumber, onion, and cilantro in a medium bowl. Squeeze in a little fresh lime juice to taste and season with salt and a pinch of white pepper. Allow the flavors to meld for about 15 minutes, then taste again, adjusting the seasoning accordingly.

Heat a grill or stovetop grill pan to medium-high. Thread the chicken strips onto bamboo skewers, using 2 strips per skewer and bunching them together. Reserve the marinade (adding a little more oil if needed) for basting. Grill the chicken skewers, turning once or twice and basting on occasion during the first 5 minutes of cooking, until the chicken is cooked through, 7 to 10 minutes.

For the salad, arrange the salad greens on 4 plates and drizzle with a little olive oil. Arrange the skewers on the greens and spoon the mango salsa on top. Serve with lime wedges and warmed corn tortillas on the side.

{ 🖾 }

MAKES ABOUT 2 CUPS

5 or 6 Roma tomatoes, finely diced
1 small red onion, finely diced
2 cloves garlic, minced
1 jalapeño chile, seeded and minced
½ bunch cilantro, leaves only
Salt
2 or 3 teaspoons lime juice (optional)

Salsa Fresca

We served this tasty salsa every day at the café with egg dishes, with tortilla chips, and on quesadillas. The Hispanic guys in the café kitchen took great pleasure in chopping and mixing all the ingredients, then teased each other over who made the best salsa.

Mix the tomatoes, onion, garlic, and chile in a bowl. Make sure you have a nice balance of colors and texture. Stir in the cilantro and a couple pinches of salt. The flavors will develop the longer it sits, and it may get hotter as well. You can stir in a little fresh lime juice for added flavor or to balance the heat.

1 or 2 chipotle chiles in adobo sauce
½ cup (1 stick) butter, room temperature
Salt
8 ears corn
Lime wedges

Roasted Corn with Chipotle Butter

In the summer at the café we roasted fresh corn, still in its husk, directly on the grill. The husks partially steamed the corn and the grilling imparted a smoky flavor. Right before they were ready, we pulled the husks back, then returned the corn to the grill for a last pass. Our staff went crazy for it, as did the guests. Chipotle chiles and adobo sauce give the flavored butter a deep, smoky taste, which compliments the roasted corn perfectly. Use freshly picked corn. The longer it sits around, the more it loses its sweetness and becomes tough.

For the chipotle butter, whirl 1 chile with a little of its sauce in a food processor, until it becomes a coarse paste. Add the butter in pieces and a pinch of salt, and process until mixed well. Taste, and if it doesn't seem spicy enough, add a little more adobo sauce, or half of another chile.

For the corn, either first peel back the husks, remove the silk, and then rewrap prior to grilling, or throw it directly on the grill as is and do those steps before serving. If you are informally grilling outdoors, your guests might like to do it themselves.

Heat a grill to medium-high. Add the ears of corn and cook, turning several times, for 10 to 15 minutes, until the husks are charred and the cobs feel tender to the touch. Transfer to a large bowl. Using a clean towel to pick up the corn, peel back the husks, leaving them intact. Throw the corn back on the grill, turning a few more times, and grill for a couple of minutes, until lightly marked and done.

Serve the ears of corn with a pinch dish of salt, the chipotle butter, and lime wedges on the side.

SERVES 4 TO 6

MINT PESTO
2 tablespoons walnuts
1 clove garlic, peeled
Pinch salt
2 tablespoons grated Parmesan or Pecorino Romano (optional)
½ cup fresh mint leaves
½ cup fresh cilantro leaves or parsley
About ½ cup olive oil

BROCHETTES
1½ pounds lamb shoulder, cut into 1-inch chunks
3 tablespoons olive oil, plus more for grilling if needed
2 sprigs fresh rosemary, stemmed and coarsely chopped
Coarse salt and freshly ground black pepper
1 sweet red bell pepper, cut into 1-inch squares
1 small onion, cut into 1-inch squares
1 lemon, halved

Rosemary Lamb Brochettes with Mint Pesto

Serve these mouthwatering lamb skewers with mint pesto on a bed of couscous, as we used to do at the café, or wrap them in warmed pita bread with a tussle of greens, chopped cucumber, and a yogurt drizzle.

For the pesto, place the walnuts, garlic, salt, and cheese in the bowl of a food processor. Pulse to combine. Add the mint and cilantro and pulse a few more times; it should still be a little chunky. Transfer to a bowl, and slowly stir in the olive oil. Taste for seasoning and add more salt if needed.

For the brochettes, place the lamb cubes in a nonreactive dish. Drizzle with the oil and sprinkle with the rosemary, salt, and pepper. Toss to coat, cover, and set aside to marinate for at least 30 minutes.

Thread the lamb pieces onto about 8 bamboo skewers, alternating with the red pepper and onion squares.

Heat a grill or grill pan to medium-high. Grill the lamb, turning every so often and basting with any remaining marinade (or using a little more olive oil, as needed) until cooked to desired doneness, about 15 minutes for medium. Just before they are ready, squeeze with lemon juice.

Serve the brochettes with the mint pesto.

1½ to 2 pounds red new potatoes, scrubbed
½ red onion
1 sweet red bell pepper
4 mushrooms
1 medium zucchini
2 or 3 ribs chard, stems and rib removed
2 tablespoons butter
2 tablespoons olive oil
Salt and freshly ground black pepper
3 or 4 eggs (1 per person)
1 cup Salsa Fresca (page 241)
Sour cream (optional)
Chopped fresh parsley or cilantro, for garnish

New Potato Hash with Poached Eggs

A café favorite since we opened, this hearty dish of sautéed potatoes and vegetables is hard to beat. Be sure to brown the potatoes well before adding all the vegetables. Cook in two pans if necessary, or make it in batches. Top with Salsa Fresca, and sour cream if desired.

Boil the unpeeled potatoes in salted water until fork tender, not soft, 20 to 25 minutes. Drain, cool, and then cut into bite-sized chunks.

Slice the onion, red pepper, mushrooms, zucchini, and chard into similar thicknesses for even cooking.

Heat the butter and olive oil in a large frying pan. Add the potatoes and a little salt and pepper and sauté until browned, about 10 minutes, shaking the pan on occasion. Add the onion, pepper, and mushrooms and cook for 2 to 3 minutes, until soft. Add the zucchini and chard and cook for 5 minutes longer, until all vegetables are nicely browned along with the potatoes. Season with a little more salt and pepper.

Poach the eggs just before hash is done. Have a medium pot of water simmering at a rapid speed. One at a time, crack the eggs into a small bowl, then gently slip them into the simmering water. Cook 2 minutes for soft yolks or longer if you like them harder. One at a time, scoop out the poached eggs with a slotted spoon and gently rest on a towel for just a second to soak up any water.

To serve, divide the hash among bowls; top each serving with a poached egg, salsa, and sour cream. Sprinkle with the parsley or cilantro to finish.

Cousins: Trevor, Nicholas, Emily, and Chi

Havrah, Richard, Josie, Leah, and Holly Christina

THE FAMILY LEGACY

My grandfather died the same week Café Kevah opened, on May 22, 1992, passing ownership of Nepenthe to his heirs. He was just shy of eighty-one years old. Daddy Bill died peacefully in his sleep from natural causes at his home in Carmel, where he lived his last few years with Alice Russell and their daughter, Havrah, as well as Alice's sister Gina and her son. Gina was his caregiver and companion.

His memorial was intimate, sweet, and impromptu, less structured or celebrated than my grandmother's but sprinkled with memorable tales and humor just the same. People gathered on the café deck after a gala fashion show in Monterey presented by my uncle Kaffe. Aunt Holly filled the back of her convertible with all the flowers and plants from the show and brought them down the coast to decorate the café. Besides our family, a few of his close friends came. Everyone milled about until one of his old buddies said, "Aren't we going to say a few words or something?" We then drew around in a circle and talked about our memories. Regardless of the lack of fanfare, he would have been pleased.

Four generations: Holly, Emily, Bill, and Erin

My grandfather's death had less impact on the day-to-day operations and overall experience at Nepenthe compared to my grandmother's passing, since he had long been living off the property, but it ended an era and solidified the authority of the next generation, giving my aunt Holly and my cousin Kirk autonomy as managers and highlighting their position as stewards of the family legacy. With his passing came a secondary transition as family members figured out their roles, if any, in the family business. Today a governing board comprises five family members who oversee the Nepenthe Corporation. My cousin Kirk and his mother, Holly, actively manage the day-to-day business along with vice president Willie Nelson, and maintain fiduciary responsibility.

MAKES 16 (2-INCH) BARS

CRUST
1 cup flour
¼ cup confectioners' sugar
Pinch salt
½ cup (1 stick) cold butter, cut into ½-inch pieces

LEMON FILLING
1¼ cups granulated sugar
¼ cup flour
4 eggs
2 teaspoons finely grated lemon zest
⅔ cup freshly squeezed lemon juice
Confectioners' sugar, for dusting

Lemony Lemon Squares

When our first café baker carried these lemon squares down the path from the prep kitchen to the café, people would clamor after him. We sold out by midday. Not only are these sunny yellow bars pretty to look at, they are a nice balance between tart and sweet. Mix it up with a blend of Meyer lemon juice and that of standard lemons, or use both lemon and lime juice for a twist on this classic.

Preheat the oven to 350°F. Line a 9-inch square baking pan with overlapping foil.

For the crust, combine the flour, confectioners' sugar, and salt in the bowl of a processor. Add the butter in pieces and pulse until it resembles coarse meal. Scrape into the pan and press evenly onto the bottom. Bake until the crust is golden brown and thoroughly cooked, 18 to 20 minutes. Remove from the oven and cool 5 minutes. Reduce the heat to 300°F.

For the filling, whisk the granulated sugar and flour in a medium bowl. Whisk in the eggs, one at a time, until smooth. Stir in the lemon zest and juice.

Pour the filling onto the still-warm crust. Bake for 20 to 25 minutes, until the filling sets and no longer jiggles in the middle. Cool completely in the pan on a rack. Gently lift out the foil liner and transfer to a board. Cut into small squares using a sharp knife. Dust with confectioners' sugar just before serving.

MAKES ABOUT 6 CUPS

2 cups whole oats
1 cup wheat flakes
1 cup raw cashews
½ cup raw sesame seeds
½ cup pumpkin seeds
⅓ cup oat bran
⅓ cup high-quality organic powdered milk
Zest of 1 orange
1½ teaspoons cinnamon
⅓ cup safflower oil
⅓ cup boiling water
⅓ to ½ cup pure maple syrup
½ cup raisins or dried cranberries

Café Kevah Granola

Low in commercial sweetener and oil, this granola is a healthy and tasty alternative to store-bought cereal. It is easy to make and stores well in a glass jar or in a resealable plastic bag in the freezer. The recipe, a variation on the one we still use at the café, can easily be doubled or tripled. Sprinkle over yogurt or serve with milk. For a sweeter granola that has more clusters, stir in ¼ cup honey with the maple syrup.

Preheat the oven to 275°F.

In a large bowl, combine the oats, wheat flakes, cashews, sesame seeds, pumpkin seeds, oat bran, powdered milk, zest, cinnamon, oil, boiling water, and maple syrup, mixing well. Spread out on a baking sheet. Bake slowly, stirring occasionally, until golden brown, 45 to 50 minutes. Stir in raisins when cooled. Store in an airtight container.

SERVES 4

APPLE PEAR BUTTER
2 baking apples, such as Gravenstein or Golden Delicious
3 yellow Bartlett pears
¾ cup apple cider or unsweetened apple juice
½ cup honey or sugar
½ cinnamon stick
1 strip lemon peel
Pinch nutmeg
Lemon juice, if needed

FRENCH TOAST
3 eggs
¾ cup buttermilk
¼ cup milk
¼ teaspoon cinnamon
¼ teaspoon ground ginger
¼ teaspoon nutmeg
½ sourdough baguette, or ½ loaf brioche-style raisin bread
2 or 3 tablespoons butter

Buttermilk French Toast with Apple Pear Butter

Another favorite at the café when we opened was our buttermilk French toast, made with thick slices of sourdough baguette or cinnamon raisin bread and topped with a lightly sweetened apple and pear butter. At the last minute, the cooked toasts are popped in the oven, giving them a final rise. The apple pear butter also comes in handy as a sweet-spicy compote to accompany a cheese plate.

For the butter, peel, core, and chop the apples and pears. Place in a heavy-bottomed pot with about ¼ cup water. Bring to a simmer and cook until the fruit is soft, about 20 minutes. Gently mash with the back of a wooden spoon. Add the honey, cinnamon, lemon peel, and nutmeg. Cook over low heat, stirring on occasion, for 20 to 30 minutes longer, until thickened and a golden hay color. Squeeze in a little lemon juice to balance the flavor, if needed. Transfer to a glass bowl and let cool. Discard the cinnamon and lemon peel. Store any extra in the refrigerator in a covered container.

For the French toast, preheat the oven to 375°F.

In a shallow bowl, whisk the eggs until frothy, then whisk in the buttermilk, milk, cinnamon, ginger, and nutmeg.

Slice the baguette on the diagonal into ¾-inch-thick slices, or the raisin bread in thick slices first, then halved on the diagonal. Drench the bread in the buttermilk batter, soaking both sides well, about minute or so total. Heat some of the butter in a large skillet over medium heat (use a lesser amount of butter to start) and cook in batches until golden brown, about 3 minutes per side.

Transfer the toasts to a baking sheet and pop them into the oven, baking until puffy and golden, about 5 minutes. Serve topped with apple butter and warmed maple syrup.

A follower of Alice Waters since high school, I tried to make a mark in my own small way by bringing in organic products, focusing on seasonal produce and sustainable food, and procuring specialty items from our backyards when possible. There wasn't anything like it at the time on the Peninsula, and we received a notable mention in an article about Big Sur in Gourmet magazine soon after.

As it turned out, quite a few people were growing food in Big Sur when we opened, and the café seemed ripe for this kind of exploration. Our salad greens came from a local farmer, hand-washed and spun right in the garden and delivered the same day. Sierra Mar at Post Ranch Inn opened around the same time, and we inevitably shared some of the same resources.

SERVES 8

STREUSEL TOPPING
¾ cup firmly packed brown sugar
½ cup flour
½ cup whole oats
2 teaspoons grated orange zest
Pinch salt
6 tablespoons cold butter

FILLING
4 heaping cups chopped rhubarb
2 heaping cups sliced plums (about 6 plums)
½ cup turbinado or firmly packed brown sugar
2 tablespoons flour
1 or 2 tablespoons fresh orange juice
1 teaspoon cinnamon

Rhubarb Plum Crisp

The bright taste of plums complements the tartness of rhubarb in this luscious fruit crisp. Crisps are a cinch to put together and can easily give or take a cup or so of fruit. I grew up making them, and they were one of the first desserts we put on the menu at Café Kevah. It is especially good with my Honey Vanilla Ice Cream (page 260). Substitute strawberries in the spring for the plums, or apples in the fall, if you wish.

Preheat the oven to 357°F.

For the streusel, combine the brown sugar, flour, oats, orange zest, and salt in the bowl of a food processor. Add the butter in pieces, pulsing until it becomes coarse crumbs.

For the filling, toss the rhubarb and plums with the turbinado sugar, flour, orange juice, and cinnamon in a large bowl, mixing well. Pour into a medium ceramic or glass casserole. Top with the streusel. Bake for 35 to 40 minutes, until bubbling and nicely browned on top. Let cool slightly. Serve with scoops of Honey Vanilla Ice Cream.

2 cups whole milk
1 cup whipping cream
½ vanilla bean
½ cup honey
4 egg yolks

Honey Vanilla Ice Cream

Honey ice cream is the perfect foil for fruit crumbles and pies, and that is how we served it at the café when we first opened. Choose a flavorful honey you enjoy eating. A dark, amber-colored wildflower honey, as we used to use, will produce an intensely flavored ice cream, a lighter one less so.

In a medium saucepan, heat the milk and ½ cup of the cream to just under a boil. Remove from the heat. Split the vanilla bean, scrape the seeds into the pot, and drop in the pod as well. Cover and let steep for 30 minutes. Stir in the honey and reheat gently until it dissolves. Don't boil or it will curdle.

Whisk the egg yolks in a small bowl. Gradually whisk in 1 cup of the warm milk to temper the egg yolks, and then pour all of it back into the pot. Cook over low heat, stirring constantly, until the custard thickens and lightly coats the back of a spoon, about 5 minutes. Place the remaining ½ cup cream in a large bowl and strain the custard into it. Whisk occasionally so a skin doesn't form as it cools. Add the vanilla pod back to the custard to continue steeping. Chill thoroughly.

Remove the vanilla bean, rinse it, and dry it overnight, then pop it in a jar of sugar to flavor it. Freeze the custard in an ice cream maker in 2 batches. Transfer the ice cream to the freezer to harden for a few hours, then let soften slightly before serving.

Raspberry Sherbet

I love how the bright, tart flavor of the raspberries shine in this sherbet, made with just a little cream to give it its smooth, creamy texture. And it's simple to make. Purée 4 cups fresh raspberries with ½ cup water until smooth; strain the mixture to remove the seeds. Stir about ⅔ cup sugar into the mixture until dissolved, and then whisk in a ¼ cup heavy cream. Freeze the sherbet in an ice-cream maker then harden in the freezer for a few hours before serving. Makes 1½ pints.

Mojave

3 cups flour
½ cup turbinado sugar
2 teaspoons baking powder
1 teaspoon baking soda
1 cup (2 sticks) cold butter, cut into small pieces
2 cups whole oats
Zest of 1 orange
¾ cup heavy cream or buttermilk
¼ cup coarse sugar or turbinado sugar, for sprinkling

Orange and Oat Scones

Years ago, when I visited the now-defunct Stars Bakery in San Francisco, I fell in love with their buttery oat scones. Back at the café, we made our own version and they were instantly a hit. Serve warm with Simple Blackberry Jam.

Preheat the oven to 350°F. Line a baking sheet with parchment paper.

Combine the flour, turbinado sugar, baking powder, and baking soda in the bowl of a food processor. Add the butter piece by piece, pulsing until pearl size. (By hand, cut the butter into the flour mixture using a pastry cutter.) Transfer the dough to a bowl and stir in the oats and orange zest. Stir in the cream until just moistened.

Bring the dough together with your hands and gently pat into an 8-inch round. Cut into triangle shapes and transfer to the prepared baking sheet, separating them so they do not touch. Sprinkle the tops with coarse sugar. Bake for 12 to 15 minutes, until lightly golden.

VARIATION: Work in 1 cup dried cranberries or golden raisins as you bring the dough together.

Simple Blackberry Jam

This is a quick, simple jam full of blackberry flavor. For about 2 cups worth, or more than enough to fill My Favorite Birthday Cake (page 210) with enough leftover for scones, start with 1 pound fresh blackberries. In a small pot, combine the blackberries with the juice and zest of 1 small orange (or other citrus) and 1¼ cups sugar. Gently stir over low heat until the sugar dissolves. Bring to a boil and cook rapidly for about 20 minutes, stirring occasionally, until the mixture thickens. Stir in a tablespoon of butter and remove from heat. The jam will set as it cools. Store in the refrigerator.

{7}

LIVING HISTORY

At the commencement of the millennium, nearly a decade after my grandfather passed and even longer since my grandmother died, Nepenthe remains grounded in the new generation. The beat era and bohemian days are a distant legacy, revered but no longer a part of the milieu. The arrival of the Internet moved us into a new age; a webcam placed on our roof gives people access to our view and once again puts us on the world stage. Today Nepenthe cultivates an award-winning wine program and a unique relationship with one of California's premier winemaker families, Pisoni Vineyards, continuing my grandparents' tradition of bridging relationships with artists and artisans and adding yet another layer to the mystique and experience at Nepenthe. It also continues the tradition of my grandmother's Sunday dinners with a smaller group of family members, now at home in the log cabin or across the way at my aunt Holly's house.

The crushing El Niño storms of 1998 closed the roads in each direction for an extended period, Nepenthe and all of Big Sur saw a surge of visitors once the roads reopened. With the emergence of a more affluent community and a broadening of theatre, art, and musical events at local venues today, Nepenthe plays host to those who revel in our lively terrace scene, with Big Sur's bohemian legacy still lurking, on the fringe. With early summer comes a stream of energy and people milling about on the coast. On the terrace are an influx of travelers and waves of families and tourists who camp at the state parks. Every August, it seems that all of Europe arrives, as many European countries offer vacation time during that month. Business remains steady throughout the year, the slower times still occurring in the winter, with heightened business around the holidays.

To run a business in Big Sur requires a wealth of support systems and people who not only know the lay of the land but also how to fix water lines and generators, run electricity, and, as in the case of the 2008 summer fires, know how to protect property and have the stamina and resources to hold their ground in the face of disaster. More than ever, Nepenthe is engaged in the process, and with an active team of managers, family involvement, and a seasoned staff on all levels, is doing well.

Nepenthe continues to surprise, offering the occasional special event, such as imaginative fire dancing by waitress Rosalia Byrne or belly dancing by my sister Sara. Singer Ledisi, a two-time Grammy nominee and part of the erstwhile Big Sur Jazz Festival, once performed to a packed house. Greek dancers from Monterey take over the dance floor annually, the lively music and dance rekindling the magic and spirit of another time.

In December 2007, our first family art show in the Phoenix Shop featured my uncle Kaffe's quilts and designs, my cousin Erin's paintings, and handcrafts and knitwear by other family members, including a beautifully crafted quilt with an Asian motif by my cousin Matthew. It is in these moments that my grandparents' legacy and our artistic heritage come to bear, unwavering and bright in the face of the ongoing challenges and complexities of growing a family business.

My family continues to create art at Nepenthe whenever we have the opportunity, building on the legacy my grandmother celebrated. In a major retrofit in 2008 that closed off part of the terrace for a couple of months, we rebuilt the outdoor fireplace with handmade bricks and added a new mosaic tabletop created by the five siblings. My sister Leah and my son Trevor both helped to lay the mosaic, a combined creative effort that represented three generations and months of planning. My uncle Kaffe (along with his assistant Brandon Mably and a team of helpers that included my son) created a mosaic of rocks and river stones, once described as a symphony of tonal grays, at the base of the retaining wall.

THE WINE PROGRAM

With over 300 selections at any given time, Nepenthe's wine list reflects the curiosity and education of my cousin Kirk, driven by years of watching, learning, and honing his palate. It also echoes our own family history, honoring small, family-owned wineries and producers who respect their land and the culture and history of their wines.

In the early days, distributors and wine salesman would come down for a whole day of eating, drinking, and selling wine on the terrace, making an event of it. We were a favorite customer because it was less a sales call than a way to join in the festivities. Kirk began buying the wine in the late 1980s, a move that crystallized his interest and passion for it.

The success of a California-wine-by-the-glass program spearheaded by manager Tom Birmingham, combined with an explosion of cult wine programs popping up across the country, helped propel Nepenthe's wine program forward. Over the years, Kirk took master classes with wine writer and educator Karen MacNeil, developing a mentor relationship with her. He attended seminars and nurtured other wine relationships (sometimes bringing the winemakers to the restaurant), most notably with Gary Pisoni. A few of Nepenthe's key waiters also took Karen's classes and passed a challenging master's test. Today, the staff "knows wine, cares about wine, and can engage about it effectively," Kirk said. We now not only have an award-winning wine list, but one that equally celebrates our unique environment and history as a family business.

ON THE MENU

Over the course of sixty years, our core menu has stayed essentially the same, with the addition of a sauce on a steak, for example, or special salad outside of the three we always served. Today, a team of trained chefs, cooks, and bakers leads the restaurant kitchen, bringing daily specials to the forefront along with new appetizers. Under the guidance of my cousin Kirk and my aunt Holly, they work to uphold the quality and care my grandparents insisted on and yet have more room to be creative, making way for the featured dishes to more readily compliment the wine program.

The Nepenthe kitchen has provided unique challenges for the creative cook, with only a singular grill with a flat griddle to service the menu, and no backup station near by or room to remodel to accommodate. We serve hundreds of lunches on a busy summer day, and it all comes from this one line. Today's lunch and dinner menu is emblematic of our original menu, featuring sandwiches, steaks, and salads, but it offers more range, occasionally highlighting local and seasonal products and consistently featuring specials.

SERVES 4

4 (6-ounce) wild salmon fillets
Sea salt
Freshly ground black pepper
Olive oil
1 lemon, sliced ¼ inch thick
Fresh California bay leaves (optional)

Grilled Wild Salmon with Lemon

In the old days Nepenthe's butcher fished on the side and often brought my grandmother the first salmon of the season, plus other fresh fish, like cod, that came from local waters. Occasionally she served the salmon at the restaurant, but mostly she reserved it for the home table.

Wild salmon is super flavorful and needs little more than a bit of seasoning and some lemon. As it cooks, toss some lemon slices on the grill and a few California bay leaves for a hint of their pungent fragrance. Pair the salmon with a simple salad as we did at the café.

Heat a grill or grill pan over medium-high heat. Season the fillets with salt and pepper, drizzle with olive oil, and set aside for 10 minutes. Gather the bay leaves if you plan to use them, gently wiping them clean.

Grill the salmon on the cooler side of the grill and turn after about 3 minutes. Cook the fish 3 to 4 minutes longer, depending on the thickness of the fillets, until opaque but still soft in the center. At the same time, grill the lemon slices and bay leaves, turning them after a couple of minutes and transferring them to a warm platter when warmed through. Arrange the fish next to the grilled lemons and bay leaves, and pass family style.

4 to 6 small or 3 large artichokes, stems trimmed
Juice of 1 lemon
2 to 3 tablespoons olive oil
Salt and freshly ground black pepper
Handful arugula or mâche (optional)
Garlic Basil Aioli (recipe follows), for serving
Lemon wedges, for serving

Grilled California Artichokes with Garlic Basil Aioli

Artichokes thrive in Monterey Country, and until the late 1990s artichoke fields flourished on both sides of the highway heading south from Carmel and down the coast. Nepenthe serves a grilled artichoke with basil aioli and a changing array of accompaniments, like butter beans tossed with herbs and olive oil, or fennel poached in olive oil with a shaved celery garnish and a balsamic reduction (pictured).

I serve artichokes on a bed of young arugula or with a few bouquets of mâche and dollops of Garlic Basil Aioli (page 276) for dipping on the side. The artichokes can be steamed several hours ahead.

Trim off the thorny tips of each artichoke and rub the cut ends with a little lemon juice. Place them cut side up in a steamer with a ½ inch of water at the bottom. Steam the artichokes, covered, over medium heat, for 20 to 25 minutes, until just tender (make sure that the water doesn't run dry). Transfer them to a towel-lined plate to drain.

Heat a grill or grill pan over medium-high heat.

When the artichokes are cool, cut them in half and discard the thistly choke, leaving the heart intact. Drizzle the artichokes with the olive oil and fresh lemon juice and season with salt and pepper. Grill over a medium-high flame, turning on occasion, until well marked and warmed through, about 5 minutes.

Arrange on plates with a tussle of arugula and dollops of the aioli. Serve with lemon wedges and the remaining aioli in a bowl for dipping.

NOTE: To make balsamic reduction, simmer ½ cup vinegar with a pinch of sugar over medium heat until reduced by half. As it cools it will become thick and syrupy.

MAKES ABOUT 1 CUP

2 cloves garlic, peeled
Salt
1 egg yolk
2 teaspoons fresh lemon juice
1 teaspoon Dijon mustard
¼ cup vegetable oil
½ cup olive oil
White pepper
2 teaspoons finely chopped basil

Garlic Basil Aioli

Along with the Grilled California Artichokes (page 275), this garlicky mayonnaise with a hint of basil is delicious with Marinated Fresh Monterey Sardines (page 110). The trick to making a good aioli is to whisk furiously as you add the oil so that it doesn't break. If it does, stop adding the oil and whisk until it comes back together. You can also make it in a food processor, stirring in a drop of water to thin.

With a fork, mash the garlic with a pinch of salt until it makes a paste. Combine half the paste with the yolk, lemon juice, and mustard in a large bowl. Combine the oils, then add a drop or two to the yolk mixture, whisking well to emulsify. Slowly add the remaining oil in a steady stream, whisking rapidly to combine. Add a pinch of white pepper and the remaining garlic, to taste, if desired. Stir in the basil.

{ 🐟 }

Roasted Garlic

Roasting whole garlic brings out its sweet flavor and mellows its pungent taste. It is great for spreading on croutons as part of an appetizer platter, along with soft goat cheese and toasted nuts, and how it is served at Nepenthe. To make, slice off the top ¼ inch of the garlic heads. Drizzle with olive oil, season with salt and pepper, and scatter with chopped fresh thyme. Bake the garlic at 375°F, covered, until soft, about 45 minutes or so.

SERVES 4

SHERRY VINAIGRETTE
1 small shallot, finely chopped
2 tablespoons sherry vinegar
1 teaspoon Dijon mustard
6 tablespoons olive oil or safflower oil
1 tablespoon water
2 teaspoons finely chopped fresh thyme
Salt and freshly ground black pepper

SALAD
8 to 12 baby golden beets (2 bunches small or 1 bunch large),
    boiled or roasted, and peeled
8 cups field greens or arugula, rinsed and crisped
½ red onion, thinly sliced
8 cherry tomatoes, halved
4 ounces fresh goat cheese, crumbled
½ cup candied pecans (see Note) or toasted pecans

Beet Salad with Sherry Vinaigrette

*The beet salad was introduced to Nepenthe's menu at the start of the new millennium,
bringing field greens to the restaurant and addressing the need for a robust salad as a
main course. The candied pecans add a hint of sweetness to the whole, but you can simply
toast them, if preferred. You can either roast the beets (see Note below) or boil them.*

To make the vinaigrette, combine the shallot, vinegar, and mustard in a small bowl.
Whisk in the oil and water. Whisk in the thyme, salt, and pepper.

For the salad, halve or quarter the beets, depending on size. Combine the beets,
greens, onion, and tomatoes in a large bowl. Toss with the vinaigrette and season
lightly with a little salt if needed. Divide among 4 plates. Sprinkle the goat cheese and
pecans over the tops and serve.

NOTE: To roast beets, throw them scrubbed but unpeeled into a baking pan and drizzle with a little olive oil.
Season with salt and pepper and add a splash of water and sherry vinegar. Cover tightly and roast at
400°F until fork tender, about 30 minutes for small ones. Peel the beets when still warm by rubbing
between two towels.

   To candy pecans, toss nuts in a sugar syrup (equal parts water and sugar/honey); add a pinch of salt and
spread them onto a lightly buttered parchment-covered pan. Bake at 300°F for about 25 minutes, until nicely
toasted and caramelized.

BROTH
1 plump whole chicken (about 3 pounds), rinsed
About 12 cups water
1 onion, quartered
2 cloves garlic, peeled
1 bay leaf

SOUP
2 tablespoons vegetable or olive oil
6 Roma tomatoes, diced
1 medium red onion, diced
1½ red sweet bell peppers, diced
1 jalapeño chile, seeded and minced
7 to 8 cups chicken broth (from above)
3 tablespoons fresh lime juice (2 or 3 limes), plus more if needed
½ bunch fresh cilantro, stemmed and chopped
2 teaspoons ground cumin
2 teaspoons salt, plus more if needed
1 teaspoon white pepper
½ cup Tomatillo Salsa (recipe follows), plus more if needed

GARNISHES
Tortilla chips
Finely chopped red onion
Shredded Monterey Jack or Cheddar cheese, or a mixture
Chopped fresh cilantro
Lime wedges

Chicken Tortilla Soup with Tomatillo Salsa

This soup was so popular at Café Kevah that we eventually served it at the restaurant, where it is still on the menu today. Much playful debate still occurs about which cook or dishwasher came up with the recipe. I always argue that it was me, they argue that it was them, but in truth it was a collaborative effort and reflected the positive, creative play that happened in the café kitchen when we had time on our hands.

It is a two-part soup, made with a whole chicken and its cooking broth, with the addition of Tomatillo Salsa to enrich the flavor. Cook the chicken up to a day ahead, and prepare the salsa ahead, too, if desired, making this soup that much easier to put together.

For the broth, place the chicken in a large stockpot and add enough cold water to cover. Bring to a boil over medium-high heat, skim off any foam, and decrease the heat to a simmer. Add the onion, garlic, and bay leaf. Simmer for 1 to 1 ½ hours, until the chicken is thoroughly cooked. Allow the chicken to cool in the broth, and then transfer it to a large bowl or baking sheet. Separate the meat from the bones, discarding the bones (or reserve for stock) and fat.

Shred the chicken and reserve for the soup. Strain the broth into another pot, skim the fat from the surface, and refrigerate unless using right away. For a richer stock, simmer the broth again, reducing it to about 8 cups.

For the soup, heat the oil in a large heavy-bottomed pot over medium-high heat. Add the tomatoes, onion, peppers, and chile and cook until soft, about 5 minutes. Stir in the broth, lime juice, cilantro, cumin, 2 teaspoons salt, and the white pepper. Bring to a boil then decrease the heat. Add the reserved shredded chicken and salsa. Simmer for about 20 minutes, until the flavors meld. Season with additional salt, adding more lime juice or salsa to taste.

To serve, ladle the soup into big bowls, making sure each has a good amount of chicken. Top with a small amount of tortilla chips, red onion, shredded cheese, and cilantro, passing lime wedges and more garnishes at the table.

NOTE: To make your own tortilla chips, cut corn tortillas into matchstick-sized strips or small triangles. Fry in hot vegetable oil until crispy, 3 to 5 minutes. Drain on paper towels and season liberally with salt.

Tomatillo Salsa

This is a versatile green salsa, excellent on eggs, as a dip for tortilla chips, or swirled into chicken broth to make our Tortilla Chicken Soup.

Place about 1 pound husked and rinsed tomatillos in a pot, cover with water, and bring to a boil. Cook until soft, about 15 minutes. Meanwhile, toast 2 chiles de arbol in a hot dry pan, turning a few times, until lightly charred. Remove the stems (shake out the seeds only if you want less heat). Drop the tomatillos, chiles, 1 chopped onion, 2 cloves garlic, and about ½ bunch stemmed cilantro in a blender, add about ⅓ cup water, and whirl until smooth. Pour into a bowl and season to taste with salt and pepper. Thin with a little more water as needed.

MAKES 1 (9-INCH) THREE-LAYER CAKE, SERVING 12

CAKE
4 ounces bittersweet chocolate, coarsely chopped
1½ cups (3 sticks) butter, cut into small pieces
1 tablespoon pure vanilla extract
3 cups flour
1 cup unsweetened natural cocoa powder
2 teaspoons baking soda
½ teaspoon baking powder
½ teaspoon salt
4 eggs
2½ cups granulated sugar
1 cup sour cream
2¼ cups milk

GANACHE
1 pound bittersweet chocolate, coarsely chopped
1 cup heavy cream

Bittersweet Chocolate Fudge Cake

This is a chocolate lover's dream: three layers of rich, fudgelike cake twice coated with bittersweet ganache for the ultimate chocolate dessert. It takes a little time to put it all together but it is worth it. At the restaurant we make two 10-inch rounds and slice them into four layers, but at home you can bake it in three 9-inch pans and stack them as is, skipping that extra step, making it that much easier and yet just as rewarding to look at and eat. Use a good quality chocolate, like Callebaut.

For the cake, preheat the oven to 350°F. Line three 9-inch round cake pans with circles of parchment paper, then butter and lightly dust with flour, knocking out any excess.

Warm the chocolate with the butter in a medium heatproof bowl set over a pot of barely simmering water, stirring on occasion, until melted. Stir in the vanilla and remove from the heat to cool.

Sift together the flour, cocoa, baking soda, baking powder, and salt into a medium bowl. Beat the eggs in an electric mixer for 2 minutes, or whisk by hand, until pale yellow. Gradually beat in the sugar until light and fluffy. Add the cooled chocolate mixture and the sour cream and beat until combined, scraping down the side of the mixing bowl to incorporate. Decrease the speed to low and alternately add the dry ingredients and the milk in 3 batches, mixing well after each addition.

Divide the batter among the prepared pans, spreading evenly with a spatula. Bake on the middle rack for 30 to 35 minutes, until a toothpick inserted in the centers comes out clean. Cool on a wire rack for 10 minutes. Run a thin knife around the edge of each layer, then invert on the rack. Remove the paper and cool completely.

For the ganache, warm the chocolate with the cream in a medium heatproof bowl set over barely simmering water, stirring occasionally, until smooth and melted. Remove from the heat and allow it to set up before using.

To frost, stack one layer on a cake round (make one out of stiff cardboard, the width of the cake), or a cake plate. Spread about ½ cup of the ganache over it. Top with a second cake layer and spread with more ganache, then top with a final layer. Spread a thinner layer of ganache on top and all around the side. Chill for 10 minutes so that the chocolate sets up and is slightly cold.

Gently warm the remaining ganache over a pot of simmering water, thinning with a little more cream if necessary. Pour it over the cake, spreading it with an offset spatula from the center out and coaxing the glaze over the sides. Use your spatula to spread it evenly all around. It is best to do this over a rack set on a small baking sheet, so that the chocolate doesn't pool up at the bottom. Let it set up for an hour or so before serving. Store at room temperature, covered with a tall cake lid if you have one.

NEPENTHE

NEPENTHE PIE DOUGH (recipe follows)

FILLING
3 cups fresh strawberries
3 cups fresh blackberries
3 cups fresh raspberries
2 tablespoons Grand Marnier
½ cup firmly packed brown sugar
¼ cup cornstarch
1½ teaspoons cinnamon

CRUMB TOPPING
⅔ cup flour
⅔ cup whole oats
⅔ cup firmly packed brown sugar
⅔ cup walnuts
½ cup (1 stick) cold butter

Nepenthe's Triple-Berry Pie

In the early 1990s we hired a chef who loved to bake, and he came up with this pie. It became an instant classic. The fruit is only lightly sweetened, and its tartness combined with the sugar-crumb topping is a perfect pairing. Served warm with vanilla ice cream, it's heavenly. If you use frozen berries, increase them by ½ cup each and defrost slightly before tossing with the other ingredients.

On a lightly floured board, roll out the dough (it may need to soften for 5 or 10 minutes first) into a 12-inch circle. Fit into a 9-inch pie pan, trim any ends hanging over the side, and flute the edge with your thumb. Chill until ready to use.

Preheat the oven to 350°F.

For the filling, wash and hull the strawberries. Cut them in half and place in a large bowl. Add the blackberries and raspberries and toss with the Grand Marnier. In a separate bowl, combine the brown sugar, cornstarch, and cinnamon. Add to the berries and gently toss.

For the topping, combine the flour, oats, brown sugar, walnuts, and butter in the bowl of a food processor. Pulse until the mixture resembles small peas. To make by hand, cut the butter into the flour and sugar, using a pastry cutter. Finely chop the walnuts and add in along with the oats.

Fill the chilled pie shell with the filling and cover thoroughly with the topping. Bake for 1 hour, until bubbling and golden brown on top.

1 cup flour
½ cup (1 stick) cold butter, cut into pieces
1 teaspoon granulated sugar
Pinch salt
1 to 2 tablespoons heavy cream

Nepenthe Pie Dough

Combine the flour, butter, sugar, and salt in a food processor and pulse until the butter resembles small peas. Drizzle in the cream a little at a time, pulsing until the dough just comes together. Add more cream if needed.

(To make by hand, cut the butter into the dry ingredients until it resembles small peas, using a pastry cutter. Sprinkle with the cream and work the dough together using a wooden spoon or rubber spatula.)

Turn the dough out onto a clean work surface and gently pat it into a flat disk. Wrap in plastic and chill for at least 30 minutes.

MAKES ENOUGH DOUGH FOR 2 (9 OR 10-INCH) PIE SHELLS

2½ cups flour
½ teaspoon salt
¾ cup (1½ sticks) cold butter, cut into 1-inch pieces
¼ cup (2 ounces) cold vegetable shortening
⅓ to ½ cup cold water

Holly's Pie Dough

Place the flour and salt in the bowl of a food processor, Add the butter and shortening and pulse until it resembles coarse meal. Sprinkle with a tablespoon of cold water and pulse, adding more water a little at a time, until the dough just comes together.

Transfer the dough to a clean work surface, and, using your fingertips, work in any loose flour, gently forming the dough into a ball. Divide it in half, pat it into 2 discs, and cover it with plastic wrap. Chill for at least 30 minutes before rolling out.

Holly and William

Trevor and Nicoya

MAKES 1 (9-INCH) PIE, SERVING 8 TO 10

½ recipe Holly's Pie Dough (page 292)

FILLING
8 Granny Smith apples, peeled and cored
Lemon juice
¾ cup firmly packed brown sugar
3 tablespoons flour
1½ teaspoons cinnamon
Dash nutmeg

STREUSEL TOPPING
1 cup flour
1 cup firmly packed brown sugar
½ cup cold butter, cut into pieces

Apple Pie with Streusel Topping

Our pies are made fresh every day in small batches with lots of love and care. My aunt Holly won first place with this pie at a benefit contest for the Apple Pie School, and she later put it on the menu at Nepenthe. The combination of tart apples in a buttery rich crust with streusel topping is a sure winner.

On a lightly floured board, roll out the dough (it may need to soften for 5 or 10 minutes first) into a 12-inch circle. Fit into a 9- or 10-inch pie pan, trim any ends hanging over the side, and flute the edge with your thumb. Chill until ready to use.

Preheat the oven to 350°F.

For the filling, slice the apples into thick wedges and place in a large bowl. Toss with a little lemon juice while preparing. Combine the brown sugar, flour, cinnamon, and nutmeg in a small bowl, add to the apples, and mix well.

For the streusel, combine the flour, brown sugar, and butter in the bowl of a food processor. Pulse until the butter resembles small peas.

Heap the filling into the prepared pie shell. Cover with the topping, packing it onto the apples. Bake for 1 hour, until the filling bubbles through the topping and the apples are tender when pricked with a fork or skewer. The apples should be tender and cooked through, with caramelized juices bubbling in the middle and at the edge of the pie.

NEPENTHE AND THE COMMUNITY

I think it is fair to say that Nepenthe is celebrated not only for its perfect location, but also for its role in feeding the community, literally and figuratively. At its start my grandparents fed people, whether friends, family, community members, visiting artists, or travelers. It was the legs they stood on, so to speak—how it all began and, unmistakably, how it has continued.

My grandparents venerated Big Sur's independent, freethinking community; involving themselves in many aspects of its growth and development over the course of their lifetimes. Since earliest memory they provided a place for artists, writers, and dancers to freely express themselves; they opened their doors to myriad performers and lecturers, offering a kind of community stage, and supported other groups over time (including the local softball team, the Outlaws). Like the European osteria and café life of the bohemian era, Nepenthe provided a welcome place for culture to unfold with great occasion and bonhomie, helping define identity in the process.

This town sure knows how to throw a disaster.

—KEN WRIGHT

To this day, Nepenthe remains a favorite gathering place. During crises it has become a site for town hall–like meetings, and community-wide feasts (In 1998, with the road closed and the power out, the restaurant threw a collective dinner where half the town showed up to share in the camaraderie.) Although there have been many changes over the years, Nepenthe's role in feeding its community has never faltered. It is at the heart of my grandparents' legacy, and our family's commitment to that tradition.

In keeping with the spirit of my grandparents' vision, Nepenthe continues to support local services, such as the Big Sur Fire Brigade, through its annual Halloween Bal Masque, and it is a major sponsor of the Big Sur River Run. Nepenthe also contributes 10 percent of its net profits to community programs that foster the arts, education, and environment.

During the Basin Complex fire (Summer 2008), which burned more than 160,000 acres, and following unprecedented road closures where locals faced arrest if caught on the highway, we kept our doors open, and a determined skeleton crew served sandwiches to fire crews and manned the phones. We experienced an outpouring of concern from all over the world, a reminder of the role Nepenthe has played in people's lives. Without power but with plenty of food and water, and a massive generator, Kirk sent word to neighbors and those risking arrest, to come and enjoy our chef's cooking. Some came by way of the canyon or staged lookouts to cross the road unhindered. "Tod [the chef] and Tom do the cooking; the rest of us clean up and share a moment's respite, tell great stories, and exchange information on the fire status," wrote Kirk in an email.

FAMILY DINNERS

The legacy of my grandmother's Sunday night dinners and the family coming together around the table continues today, whether at home or in the restaurant. For many years, my aunt Holly held weekly dinners at her house, around that same family table, and now they take place at my cousin Kirk's house or at Erin's in the log cabin. Unlike my grandmother's dinners, they don't have a large extended following and are usually limited to family and close friends, depending on who is in town. Whenever I am there with my children, we gladly take up the invitation. At the restaurant we pile around the half-round tables in good cheer, grateful for the familial and creative heritage that binds. At home, connections deepen in the kitchen, where each person contributes to the meal. Meredith might make her fabulous Summer Garden Salad, Tom prepares a main dish or something to accompany, such as his Piquant Cornbread, and Holly always makes a dessert. Kirk brings the wine, my cousin Erin might bring a loaf of her sourdough bread, made with a natural starter, and others like myself usually fill in with an appetizer. Regardless of the location or time of year, the breaking of bread and fellowship remains a heartened memory and beloved family tradition.

SERVES 8

1 cup yellow cornmeal
1 cup flour
1 or 2 tablespoons granulated sugar or honey
2 teaspoons baking powder
1 teaspoon baking soda
1 teaspoon chili powder
½ teaspoon ground cumin
1 teaspoon salt
1 egg, whisked
⅓ cup vegetable oil
¾ cup buttermilk
½ cup milk
½ cup loosely packed fresh cilantro leaves, finely chopped
½ white onion, finely diced
½ sweet red bell pepper, finely diced
1 jalapeño chile, seeded and minced
1 cup shredded sharp Cheddar cheese

Tom's Piquant Cornbread

Over the years, Tom Birmingham has contributed many recipes to Christmas dinners and Sunday night dinners at home, and to this day he still cooks the holiday meal for Nepenthe, its staff, and families. Moist and quite tasty, this piquant cornbread goes well with many dishes, like Dotty's Baked Ham with Mustard Glaze-Brown Sugar (page 94).

Preheat the oven to 400°F. Lightly grease an 8-inch square baking pan.

Combine the cornmeal, flour, sugar, baking powder, baking soda, chili powder, cumin, and salt in a large mixing bowl. Whisk the egg with the oil in a small bowl, and then stir into the dry mixture. Stir in the buttermilk, milk, cilantro, onion, red pepper, chile, and cheese until thoroughly combined.

Pour into the prepared pan and bake for 25 minutes, until a toothpick inserted in the center comes out clean.

DRESSING
½ cup fruity extra virgin olive oil
Good-quality aged red wine vinegar
Balsamic vinegar
Juice of 1 lemon (optional)
Sea salt and freshly ground black pepper

SUMMER SALAD
4 ears fresh corn (yellow and white), shucked
4 or 5 ripe heirloom tomatoes, cut into wedges
1 basket red and yellow cherry tomatoes, each halved
1 bunch fresh basil, rinsed and patted dry
2 avocados, peeled, pitted, and cut into chunks
2 or 3 large handfuls salad greens (such as mâche, oak leaf,
    and/or spinach), rinsed and spun dry
6 to 8 ounces chilled fresh goat cheese, preferably Laura Chenel's

Meredith's Summer Garden Salad

Meredith's salad of fresh corn, avocado, and vine-ripened tomatoes is a favorite combination of mine. Her dressing is especially delicious.

This recipe is more of a guide than anything else. Allow yourself to wander the market and choose vegetables at the height of their seasons. The corn should be just picked, stored no more than a day or two, and the tomatoes ripened on the vine. Use the best fruity extra virgin olive oil that you can afford and good-quality vinegar.

For the dressing, in a glass jar with a tight-fitting lid, combine the olive oil with an equal amount of vinegars and/or lemon juice. Add a "palm full of salt [a tablespoon or so] and a few grindings of pepper," as Meredith says. Secure the lid and shake vigorously. Taste for seasoning.

For the salad, using a sharp, heavy knife, shave the corn kernels from the cobs into a large salad bowl. Break up the corn with your fingers and remove any silk threads. Add the heirloom and cherry tomatoes to the corn. Stem the basil leaves and add in whole, along with the avocados and greens. Gently toss to combine. Separate the goat cheese into smaller clumps with a fork, and add to the salad. Add dressing to taste and toss to coat. Check for seasoning, making adjustments as needed.

MAKES 1 (8 OR 9-INCH) TART, SERVING 8 TO 10

SWEET DOUGH
½ cup (1 stick) butter, softened
4 tablespoons confectioners' sugar
Pinch salt
1 cup flour

LEMON CURD
5 or 6 Meyer lemons (about 1 cup juice)
3 eggs plus 3 egg yolks
⅞ cup granulated sugar, or to taste
4 tablespoons butter

Meyer Lemon Tart

A lemony custard tart is always a crowd pleaser and looks beautiful on display. It is often made around the holidays at the restaurant and is one of my most favorite desserts to make at home. The sweet dough crust is easy and simply pressed into the pan, making it a snap to put together.

To make the dough, beat the butter with the sugar, salt, and flour until just combined. Press the dough evenly into a 9-inch round fluted tart pan. Freeze the prepared tart shell for at least 30 minutes before baking.

Meanwhile, make the lemon curd. Zest half the lemons (setting the zest aside), then extract the juice from all the lemons to make about 1 cup. In a medium nonreactive, heatproof bowl, whisk the eggs and sugar until well combined, then whisk in the lemon juice.

Place the bowl over a gently simmering pot of water and whisk continuously until it begins to thicken, about 5 minutes. Whisk in the butter in pieces; cook, stirring frequently, until the curd coats the back of the spoon, another 5 minutes or so. This is a good time to taste and adjust the sweetness, as needed.

Strain the curd into a separate bowl, then whisk in the zest. Press a piece of plastic wrap on the surface while cooling.

Preheat the oven to 375°F.

Bake the tart shell for 20 to 25 minutes until golden brown. Cool slightly, then spoon the lemon curd into the shell, spreading evenly with a spatula. Bake for 7 to 10 minutes, until just set but still slightly jiggly in the middle.

Serve chilled with a dollop of lightly whipped cream or with fresh berries.

EMPLOYEE MEALS

For years and years the family kitchen at Nepenthe provided not only a meal for staff, but also a place to unwind between shifts and to catch up with friends. The employee meals, occurring twice a day, were boisterous gatherings around my grandmother's dinner table in the upstairs kitchen. It was a time for staff to slow down long enough to catch a breath before the curtain call, a time for sharing stories and staying abreast of each other's lives. These shared meals were a huge part of the experience of working there and were sorely missed when the kitchen closed down.

All Nepenthe and Phoenix Shop employees today receive a shift meal, and though there is no longer a family table upstairs to eat around and time is more limited, staff still gather to eat and talk, and to compose themselves for the day's work ahead. At 11:00 a.m., just prior to the 11:30 opening, the restaurant day staff, including gardeners and maintenance people, come together around a table for repast. Typically they order off the grill, since we no longer have a family cook. On occasion, Javier Perez Rubalcava, our longtime cook, and kitchen supervisor, brings to life this Nepenthe tradition and makes a special meal for all to enjoy. His Chile Rellenos (page 306) are particularly revered.

The Hispanic Community

Hispanic workers have been a major influence on the restaurant over the past twenty years, filling the usual gap of available employees during our busiest season and providing us with a stronger ground crew year to year. Transient labor, while typical in years past, is now often replaced with local youth, children of long-term employees, and a solid, enthusiastic bilingual community. For Nepenthe, their contribution has been immeasurable, providing us with a pool of eager crew members who are devoted and consistent. Many have moved into more solid positions in the kitchen and management, adding a welcome, cultural dimension to our staff and giving new meaning to the idea of extended family. Some employees have been with us since their youth, some have returned to their home countries and stay in touch, and others have opened their own businesses, serving our community at large.

TOMATO ONION SAUCE

4 or 5 large tomatoes, coarsely chopped,
    or 1 (28-ounce) can tomatoes, with juice
½ yellow onion, diced; plus 4 yellow onions, sliced
5 cloves garlic
1 whole clove, or a pinch ground cloves
Pinch dried Mexican oregano
1 or 2 chiles de arbol, stemmed
1 guajillo chile, stemmed and torn into pieces
Salt and freshly ground black pepper
3 tablespoons vegetable or olive oil

CHILE RELLENOS

Safflower or canola oil, for frying
12 fresh poblano or pasilla chiles, preferably with long stems
1½ pounds mozzarella or Mexican-style cheese, grated
5 eggs, separated, plus 3 egg whites
Pinch salt
1½ cups flour, for dredging

Javier's Chile Rellenos

Javier Perez Rubalcava started working at Café Kevah as a young, shy fifteen-year-old, and has since worked his way up to the restaurant kitchen. Today he is kitchen supervisor and knows all that goes on with food at Nepenthe. A couple of times a month he cooks a family-style meal for staff, and everyone goes crazy for his chile rellenos. They are a bit of a process, so plan ahead, making them in two or three steps.

For the sauce, place the tomatoes, the diced ½ onion, garlic, clove, oregano, chiles, salt, and pepper in a blender with about ½ cup water (none if using canned tomatoes), and puree until smooth.

Heat the oil over medium-high heat in a large pot. Add the sliced onions and sauté until lightly caramelized, about 10 minutes. Pour in the tomato mixture and simmer for 20 to 30 minutes. Season to taste with more salt and pepper. The sauce should be thin and brothlike. Add more water as needed.

For the chile rellenos, heat 1 inch of oil in a wide, heavy pot to 350° to 375°F. The oil should be shimmering on the surface but not smoking. In three batches, fry the chiles, turning them continuously, for about 1 minute, until evenly blistered. Drain on paper towels. Remove the oil from the heat.

When the chiles are cool enough to handle, rub off the skins, and make a slit on one side of each, starting ½ inch or so below the stem and to within ½ inch of the tip. Carefully pull out all the seeds. Rinse the chiles under cool water and drain on paper towels, slit side down.

Stuff the chiles with the cheese, being careful not to tear open the slit. Gently squeeze the chile to close. You can prepare the chiles up to this point and refrigerate for up to 1 day.

Reheat the oil to 350° to 375°F.

Meanwhile, beat the egg whites in a large bowl with a pinch of salt until fairly stiff. Whisk in the yolks, one at a time, and beat until thoroughly incorporated. Set up an assembly line near the stove with the flour in a bowl or flat dish and the egg batter in the large bowl. Roll a stuffed chile in the flour, shaking off any excess. Holding the stem, dip the chile in the egg batter, then immediately slip it into the hot oil. Repeat with 3 more chiles. Fry the chiles until golden on one side, 3 to 4 minutes, spooning a little oil onto the tops as the bottoms cook. Gently turn the chiles over with metal tongs, frying the other side until golden. Transfer the chiles to a paper towel–lined tray to drain. Repeat with the remaining chiles. (Keep the egg batter in the refrigerator between batches.)

At this point, you can either serve the chiles right away with the sauce or hold them to serve later, reheating them in the oven. This last step renders some of the grease and ensures the chiles are evenly warmed through. To reheat the chiles, fit them snugly into a baking dish and place in a 350°F oven for about 15 minutes.

Javier's father, Bonifacio, was a dishwasher at the restaurant when Javier started at the café, and was famed for his Chicken Caldo, a humble soup he whipped up between duties. It consisted of two or three half chickens, a head of celery, a few carrots, onions, lots of garlic, chiles, tomatoes, lemon, and cilantro, made over the course of the morning, and served with his own fiery salsa.

To serve, bring the tomato onion sauce back to a simmer and taste for seasoning, adding salt if needed. Remember, the sauce should be fairly thin. Place 1 or 2 chiles on each plate and cover with the sauce.

NOTE: Chiles de arbol are small, bright red dried chiles that are hot, so use sparingly or substitute with a pinch of cayenne pepper. The guajillo chile is mild to moderately hot and has shiny, smooth reddish brown skin. You can also use the even milder New Mexico chile.

Pisoni
Vineyards

A FAMILY VINEYARD

The Pisoni Vineyards & Winery property nestles against the Santa Lucia range, the angular stretch of mountains separating the fertile Salinas Valley from the Pacific Ocean. The Santa Lucia Highlands, now its own appellation, and just over the hill from Nepenthe as the crow flies, provide ideal growing conditions for cool-weather varietals such as Pinot Noir and Chardonnay.

Gary Pisoni, wild man and visionary of the family business, is known as much for his unusual vineyard practices that produce some of California's most sought-after wines as for his huge personality and jubilant storytelling. One story is about stuffing a particular Burgundian vine cutting into his pants for a cross-Atlantic plane ride home that raised eyebrows at customs and in the wine world. He tells of boyhood travails as the son of vegetable farmers and his first winemaking experiments, winning an award at the country fair years before he was even old enough to drink. Gary's parents, Eddie (recently deceased) and Jane Pisoni, farmed for over sixty years, both of them born and raised in the Salinas Valley and of Swiss Italian descent.

Pisoni Vineyard is a necessity of life for me.

—GARY PISONI

With over twenty years of experience growing Pinot grapes, Gary oversees all aspects of the grape growing and has his hand in making the wine. He favors the alignment of stars and his sense of taste to determine the ripeness of fruit and time for picking and is almost always right, according to his son Mark, who manages the day-to-day operations for both Pisoni Farms and Pisoni Vineyards. His youngest son, Jeff, crafts the wine. Gary's mother still does the books, and his father advised on the farming. Like Nepenthe, Pisoni Farms & Vineyards is three-generation family-run, and they intend it to be around for the next generation.

Gary and Kirk

Being there feels like I've landed in an oasis in the middle of dusty Steinbeck country, but in actuality the small farming town of Gonzales is just yonder, Salinas perhaps an hour away at most, and the breezy Monterey Peninsula just a morning's leisurely drive. It is honest country, lean and rugged with miles of farmlands stretching east to the velvet Gabilan Mountains. The craggy Santa Lucias form the western slopes, and together they frame California's most lucrative agriculture valley. The land is rich with history and Pisoni family lore, having first been the family's cattle ranch, where water had to be trucked in for irrigation until they found a water source, nearly ten years later. The Pinot grapes thrive in such a location, benefiting from the decomposed soil, wind-driven winters, low fog, and cool, marine temperatures that roll in most mornings and nights.

The Pisoni property, an outcrop edged by ancient oaks and native scrub, shares the land with pigs, bobcats, and other wild animals. At a clearing at the end of the road lies an outdoor kitchen under a gazebo-like frame. There is a pond and makeshift diving board, a row of apple trees with crisp, bright apples, and a wooden bathhouse on a hill overlooking all. A carpet of well-tended grapes grows on the hilly slopes below, overlooking the vast valley lands, providing a verdant calm amid the rocky terrain. At least once a year, the Pisoni family hosts a barbecue for Nepenthe staff here, and other times they head out for visits on their own.

Years ago, after visiting Gary's property along with some of Nepenthe's staff and a dozen sommeliers from around California, my cousin Kirk immediately

Aengus

hit it off with Gary, and the relationship between Nepenthe and Pisoni blossomed. In 2002, Gary invited Nepenthe to make Pinot Noir wine with grapes harvested from Garys' Vineyard (a collaboration between Gary Pisoni and Gary Francioni, and just down the road a few miles). Nepenthe couldn't sell it based on complications surrounding where it was bottled (at home), so Gary gave the restaurant and our staff thirty cases instead. "It was really the nexus of the relationship," said Kirk, who has nurtured not only a business relationship, but also a close friendship with the family ever since.

Recently we held a celebration at the restaurant in honor of the Pisoni family, featuring a three-course gourmet dinner by chef Tod Williamson (including Nepenthe-grown cherry tomatoes in a gazpacho shooter) and crew, with a rustic, plum-raspberry tart to finish. As far as we know, Nepenthe was the first to create a page on our wine list, dubbed Garys' World, that highlights twelve California artisan winemakers that use grapes grown specifically for them by both Gary Pisoni and Gary Francioni, as well as other wines made by their individual estates. The restaurant sells more of Lucia, the Pisoni sister label, than any other restaurant in the nation. Earthy, full bodied, and ripe with lush, spicy fruit, it is the darling of the staff.

More than a year after my initial visit to the vineyard, I attended the 2008 harvest at Garys' Vineyard, arriving at 5:00 a.m. with photographer Sara Remington and her boyfriend, Tim, a chef. Workers, including several women, moved at rapid speed through the rows of grapes, trimming them, dropping them into square boxes, and then chucking the deep, purple bunches into larger bins in the back of a slowly moving tractor, where several more workers sorted and disposed of debris. Later I tasted grapes that were a separate allocation just for Nepenthe, designated to make the Lucia wine that we will sell in 2010, just short of having our own private label.

Aengus Wagner, a longtime waiter at Nepenthe and a childhood pal, who has also nurtured a close relationship with the family, summed up the Pisoni philosophy. "From the ground up and throughout the wine world, the Pisonis' skills [as growers and winemakers] and passion for family is only to be exceeded by their generosity and spirit," he said. This reflects our own family traditions and history and what we hope to convey and share with our guests at Nepenthe.

SWEET DOUGH
1¼ cups flour
3 tablespoons confectioners' sugar
Pinch salt
½ cup (1 stick) cold butter, cut into small pieces
2 or 3 tablespoons heavy cream or water

PLUM FILLING
2 tablespoons raw almonds, finely chopped
   (or 3 tablespoons crushed amaretti cookies)
7 tablespoons granulated sugar
5 or 6 ripe plums, pitted and sliced into wedges
1 cup raspberries
2 tablespoons butter, cut into pieces
2 tablespoons milk, for brushing
2 tablespoons coarse sugar (optional)
Plum or raspberry jam, for brushing (optional)

Rustic Plum Raspberry Tart

The beautiful deep ruby color and sweet, tart taste of ripe plums stand out in this rustic tart. The edges of the dough are folded over the fruit filling, similar to the French galette. Serve with Honey Vanilla Ice Cream (page 260).

For the dough, mix together the flour, confectioners' sugar, and salt in a medium bowl. Cut in the butter using 2 forks or a pastry cutter, until the butter resembles small peas. Stir in the cream until the dough just comes together. Pat into a disc and refrigerate for 30 minutes.

Roll the dough out into a 12-inch circle on a lightly floured board. Carefully transfer to a parchment paper–lined baking sheet.

Preheat the oven to 375°F.

For the filling, stir together the almonds and 1 tablespoon granulated sugar and sprinkle on the surface of the dough, leaving a 1½ to 2-inch border all the way around. Pile the plums into the middle and scatter the raspberries on top. Sprinkle with the remaining granulated sugar and dot with the butter. Fold the edge of the dough in over the outer edge of the plums, pleating loosely. Brush the top of the crust with the milk and sprinkle with coarse sugar.

Bake for 50 minutes, until the crust is browned and the fruit is bubbling. Brush the fruit with its own juices or warm jam thinned with a little water, while still hot.

Holly, Kirk, and William

Nepenthe is a wonderful and dynamic business in an extra-ordinary location that provides for our family, and gives us the opportunity to serve our community and guests from all around the world. To be stewards of such a unique property and to be able to share it with the rest of the world for generations to come is a great honor and privilege.

—KIRK GAFILL

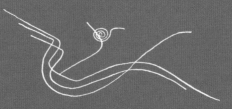

Epilogue

This past summer I spent two weeks in the log cabin, waking early to sit at the window that overlooks the terrace, the soft light glimmering through the lace curtains, teasing the painting-covered walls. It is the same spot from which my grandmother watched Nepenthe's daily unfolding, spread out on her big bed surrounded by balls of yarn, fabric, letters, and books, and where she received guests. It is the room where memories surface, where the creak in the floorboards conjure my grandmother coming in and out of her bedroom, the heavy slap of her sandals on the bare planks, the clank of the thumb handle as she closed the door to her private room.

Now my cousin Erin and her husband, Tom, live here, where she paints and writes, and where they raised their family. I watch the dense carpet of fog swirl in and out over the landscape, briefly revealing a swath of warm blue sky, only to cover it up again within moments. Typical summer, I think.

I take comfort in watching Luis and his crew on the deck each day, wiping down tables, organizing the chairs and stacking pillows, sweeping the debris, and generally preparing the restaurant to open, as he has for years. Before Luis it was Jamal, faithful in his sameness, early morning after morning into day, a figure in my children's youth and in my own.

Below on the terrace, I can hear the delighted voice of young William, my cousin Kirk's son, named after my grandfather, who has just been designated his father's chief assistant. He giggled when he told me this, a gleeful "Yeah, like, can you believe it?" laugh. He takes his new position seriously, walking around the property with pencil and pad in hand, a pager on his belt. William is barely six years old.

Watching him I am reminded of the many hours we spent following in our grandparents' footsteps learning the ropes: rolling out the fire hoses once a year, counting money in the office, tallying the daily meals, and working our first paid jobs (mine was as a dishwasher). How proud we were to be a part of the family business.

Growing up at Nepenthe was not insignificant. There is no map that can detail such a life, the intricate web of restaurant activity mixed with family; the interconnected stories; the mad splash of creativity, exploring, and hand making; the friends on horseback festooned in silver and leather chaps arriving on Sunday afternoons; the juggler, dancer, musician, and myriad friends and friends of friends.

The events behind the scenes, some days, could be just as exciting as what was going on at the restaurant below. With many people living on the property, a kind of campus atmosphere evolved, with a central family kitchen where people cooked and ate together daily. That kitchen was an extension of my grandmother's home and the center of our world outside of the restaurant.

As the business matured after my grandmother died, rules for residing on the property changed, and despite what was beloved then, they made it a better and safer place to live today. Perhaps the biggest change was when the family kitchen closed. Each house and room now has its own cooking facility and is independent of the restaurant.

Many of the old cabins have been remodeled, and a few of the rooms have been turned into offices. Some who live on the property have created private sanctuaries for themselves with thriving gardens and artful outdoor spaces. In the rustic board and batten house that I grew up in on the lower property, one of our waitresses nurtures a stunning rose garden and holds dinner parties on the lawn where our bathhouse used to be. Next door, my cousin's wife, Meredith, grows a jumble of flowers, herbs, tomatoes, and vine-squash on a small hillside plot. A rambling blackberry bush climbs up the fence, and mosaic stepping-stones lead the way to their house. Other houses edge the glossy seaside; the tops of trees tumble below their view shed, rewarding residents with a million-dollar expanse.

My grandmother's private garden in front of the cabin has been transformed with perennials, old-fashioned climbing roses, a Japanese maple, and a Meyer lemon tree. The stake fencing stands by sheer will and the weight of ivy and grapevines tangled together.

Today at Nepenthe a jolt of creativity stirs in the background, and the community is fervent and enthusiastic. With all its years, the restaurant runs smoothly, but not a day goes by when there isn't something that needs attention, whether it's a scheduling issue, the computer system going down, a delivery truck needing help getting up or down the narrow road, the water line breaking, or a customer who needs a little gas to make it down the highway. The beauty of Nepenthe is that for all that has changed, it is much the same, too.

THE
AGE OF
FABLE

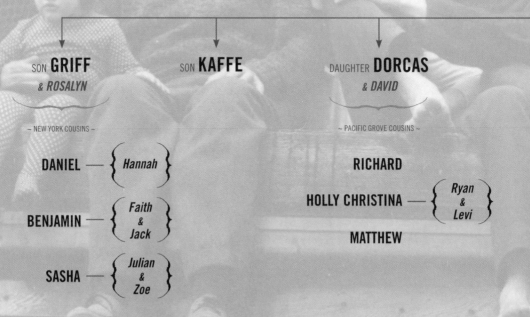

BILL'S GRANDFATHER
WILLIAM ELLIOT GRIFFIS
↓

LOLLY'S GRANDPARENTS
FRANK HUBBARD POWERS
& *JANE GALLATIN*
↓

MOTHER
KEVAH (LILLIAN EYRE GRIFFIS)
& *EDWARD LEE McCALLIE*
& *later* *NEWTON FASSETT*

MOTHER
GRACE MADELEINE
"NONA" POWERS
& *SETH ULMAN*
↓

LOLLY'S SISTER
ELIZABETH

HEIDI McGURRIN

~ SYCAMORE CANYON COUSINS ~
{ **THYME, WINONA, ALISTAIR** }
↓
Mojave, Ceiba

SON **GRIFF**
& *ROSALYN*

SON **KAFFE**

DAUGHTER **DORCAS**
& *DAVID*

~ NEW YORK COUSINS ~

DANIEL — { *Hannah* }

BENJAMIN — { *Faith* & *Jack* }

SASHA — { *Julian* & *Zoe* }

~ PACIFIC GROVE COUSINS ~

RICHARD

HOLLY CHRISTINA — { *Ryan* & *Levi* }

MATTHEW

Lolly, Erin, Bill, Cap, Kaffe, Kim, Nani as baby, Kirk, Holly, and Dorcas, 1966

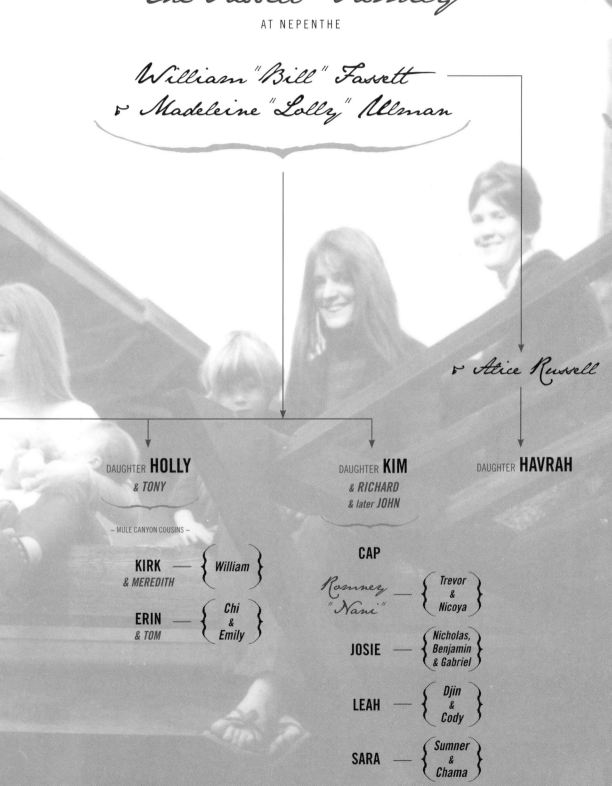

The Fassett Family

AT NEPENTHE

William "Bill" Fassett
& Madeleine "Lolly" Ullman

& Alice Russell

DAUGHTER **HOLLY**
& *TONY*

DAUGHTER **KIM**
& *RICHARD*
& later *JOHN*

DAUGHTER **HAVRAH**

~ MULE CANYON COUSINS ~

KIRK — { *William* }
& *MEREDITH*

ERIN — { *Chi* & *Emily* }
& *TOM*

CAP

Romney "Nani" — { *Trevor* & *Nicoya* }

JOSIE — { *Nicholas, Benjamin & Gabriel* }

LEAH — { *Djin* & *Cody* }

SARA — { *Sumner* & *Chama* }

Nepenthe Time-Line

1906	FIRST AUTOMOBILE MAKES IT AS FAR AS THE POST RANCH, OVER THE OLD ROAD.
1920s	SAM TROTTER BUILDS THE LOG CABIN. GREAT-GRANDFATHER FRANK POWERS DIES.
1929	GRANDMOTHER LOLLY DEPARTS FOR CAPRI.
1935	GRANDPARENTS BILL AND LOLLY FASSETT MARRY.
1936	UNCLE GRIFF IS BORN.
1937	THE COAST HIGHWAY OFFICIALLY OPENS. UNCLE KAFFE IS BORN.
1939	DEETJEN'S OPENS AS A RESTAURANT.
1941	AUNT DORCAS JANE IS BORN.
1943	AUNT HOLLY IS BORN.
1944	HENRY MILLER MOVES TO BIG SUR. ORSON WELLES BUYS THE PROPERTY FOR RITA HAYWORTH. GREAT-GRANDMOTHER JANE POWERS DIES IN ROME.
1946	MOTHER KIM IS BORN.
1947	OUR FAMILY PURCHASES NEPENTHE PROPERTY.
1949	NEPENTHE OPENS.
1950s	FIRST BAL MASQUE.
1957	PAY PHONE INSTALLED ON THE RAMP LEADING UP FROM THE PARKING LOT.
1959	HEARST CASTLE OPENS. GRANDFATHER BILL OPENS RESTAURANT IN MONTEREY, CLOSES SAME YEAR.
1960s	ASTROLOGY PARTIES BEGIN, FIRST FOR EMPLOYEES THEN EXPANDED TO THE PUBLIC.
1961	COUSIN KIRK GAFILL IS BORN.
1962	ESALEN INSTITUTE OPENS ITS DOORS, FORMERLY SLATE'S HOT SPRINGS.
1963	COUSIN ERIN GAFILL IS BORN.
1964	PHOENIX SHOP OPENS. BROTHER CAP IS BORN. FILMING OF *THE SANDPIPER*.
1965	I AM BORN. WORLD SCREENING OF *THE SANDPIPER* IN CARMEL. UNCLE KAFFE MOVES TO LONDON. THE DARK ANGEL, BY BUZZ BROWN, IS INSTALLED ABOVE THE PHOENIX SHOP. *LATE 1960s* DIONNE WARWICK AND PERCY SLEDGE PERFORM ON THE TERRACE. GRANDFATHER BILL TRAVELS TO LONDON TO VISIT KAFFE. MARY BELLE SHELD IS HIRED TO MANAGE THE RESTAURANT AND MOVES ONTO THE PROPERTY WITH HER DAUGHTER TINA. ALICE RUSSELL ARRIVES, BECOMES MANAGER AT THE PHOENIX SHOP. FASHION SHOWS RESUME. THE MAHARISHI MAHESH YOGI IS CARRIED ACROSS THE TERRACE ON A PLATFORM FILLED WITH FLOWERS.
1970s	FASHION SHOW IS HELD WITH UNCLE KAFFE'S DESIGN. THE JUICE BAR OPENS. MY MOTHER MARRIES. MY THREE SISTERS ARE BORN, AS IS HAVRAH, MY GRANDFATHER'S DAUGHTER WITH ALICE RUSSELL. AUNT HOLLY ASSUMES ROLE AS RESTAURANT MANAGER.
1976	PHOENIX BIRD SCULPTURE IS INSTALLED ON THE TERRACE.
1980	CAFÉ AMPHORA OPENS.
1983	COUSIN ERIN MARRIES FUTURE MANAGER TOM BIRMINGHAM.
1985	COUSIN KIRK ASSUMES ROLE AS GENERAL MANAGER, WHILE HOLLY IS ON LEAVE.
1986	GRANDMOTHER LOLLY DIES. COUSIN ERIN AND I RETURN TO NEPENTHE.
1987	I MARRY.
1989	TOM BIRMINGHAM BECOMES RESTAURANT MANAGER.
1991	SON TREVOR IS BORN.
1992	CAFÉ KEVAH AND THE POST RANCH INN (SIERRA MAR RESTAURANT) OPENS. GRANDFATHER BILL DIES.
1993	DAUGHTER NICOYA IS BORN.
1998	EL NINO CLOSES HIGHWAY 1 FOR THREE MONTHS AND NEPENTHE CLOSES TOO.
2000	WEBCAM DEBUTS ON THE ROOF. ENHANCED WINE PROGRAM BEGINS.
2002	NEPENTHE STAFF MAKES WINE WITH THE PISONI FAMILY.
2008	BIG SUR FIRES. FILMING BEGINS FOR JACK KEROUAC DOCUMENTARY. REBUILDING OF FIREPLACE AND OUTDOOR MOSAIC.
2009	NEPENTHE'S 60TH ANNIVERSARY.

Stage Notes

My sincere thanks to the following people:

To everyone at Andrews McMeel Publishing for your enthusiasm and kind reception, especially my editor, Jean Lucas, for guiding this project to fruition; and Kirsty Melville for understanding my book right away, and taking it under her wing.

To my mentor, Dianne Jacob, for your astute editing, guidance, and wonderful friendship. To my agent, Carole Bidnick, for championing my book, words of encouragement, and for keeping me on track.

To Sara Remington, for your beautiful photography, dedication, and vision. This book is as much yours as it is mine.

To Kodiak Greenwood for the exquisite cover photo.

To Tina Snow, childhood friend and styling assistant, for staying the course and caring so much. To Carol Hacker of Table Prop in San Francisco for generous use of props.

To Lisa Berman, my book designer and good friend, for your exquisite eye and appreciation of Nepenthe's unique story (and to Ryk and Harlan, too), and for working so hard on this book.

Thanks also to my family: To my cousin Kirk Gafill and my aunt Holly Fassett especially, who run Nepenthe and who at every turn have given support and paved the way for this book to happen. To my mother Kim Fassett Rowe, uncles Kaffe Fassett and Griff Fassett, and my aunt Dorcas Owens, for believing in my project at its onset, and so willingly sharing your stories and offering encouragement. To Kaffe, also, for contributing fabrics. And to my aunt Rosalyn Fassett for her wedding story.

Thanks to my sisters Josie, Leah, and Sara, and brother Cap, for your friendship and support; to my cousin Holly Christina Rose, for showing up in the rain at the photo shoot; and to Meredith Gafill for always offering a hand and contribution of flowers for the Pisoni dinner. To my daughter Nicoya, niece Chama, and nephews Sumner, Djin, and Cody, and my little cousins William and Mojave, for being willing subjects in my book. And to my cousin Winona Lewis and her husband, John Lovell, for your meaningful friendship and testing and tasting recipes. To my cousin Erin Gafill and her husband, Tom Birmingham, for so much, not least opening your home time and again; and to Tom also for scanning images and providing a recipe.

Special acknowledgment and thanks to Willie Nelson, for your service to our family and for being so quick to respond to and answer questions. You are the best.

Thanks to the entire staff at Nepenthe, the Café Kevah, and the Phoenix Shop for making Nepenthe the wonderful place it is today. A special thanks to Javier Perez Rubalcava, for cooking and preparing much of the food we photographed, and more. To Felipe Martinez for insights and memories of our time working together. To chef Tod Williamson, sous-chef Christian Fenton, and manager Tim Tavolara, and the restaurant and café kitchen crews and bakers for working around us and offering help when needed; as well to the chefs for that wonderful meal for the Pisoni dinner; and to Chris, also, for your help with recipes.

Special thanks to the Pisoni family for your part in this book, and especially for sharing so much of what you do with all of us.

To Mary Belle Snow, for your insight into the '60s at Nepenthe and your and Tom's hospitality.

For creative support, thank you to Gwen Meyer for storyboard advice, to Todd Koons for a much-needed laptop, to my son Trevor for building my first Web site, and technical support, to Heike Liss for initially imagining this book with me, to Alice Medrich for your suggestions on how to organize my manuscript, to

Deborah Madison for writing guidance, to Sue Conley for encouraging me in this direction early on, and to Dominique DaCruz for long ago suggesting I do something with my words, and for early encouragement on this book.

To all my interview subjects and those who helped fill in the blanks, my gratitude: Steve Copeland, Sylvia Rudolph, Byron Rudolph, Peter Monk, Herb Evans, Erica Weston, Tenny Chonin, Helen Morgenrath, Steve Bowers, Jill Bowers, Clovis Harrod, Ronni DeCarlo, John Lamore, Stefano Cacace, Linda Grant, Sally Wylie, Bill Worth, Guy Lawlor, Rita Gatti, Ken Wright, Caryl Hill, Jeremy Slate, Greg Nelson, Hope Gallop, Aengus Wagner, Bob Trezise, Irene Masteller, Mark Hudson, Jacci Pappas, and the late Bob Skiles; cousins Tony Orser, Gretchen McCausland, Joy D'Ovidio, and Heidi McGurrin. Thanks to Cynthia Williams for planting the seed; Constanzo and Titina Vuotto for sharing stories and recipes from Capri; and Perla Armanasco for the video clip of my grandfather. Thank you also to my grandfather's oldest friends: Bill Stewart, Buck Bemis, Howard Brunn, and Richard de Mille. And thank you to all who responded to my call for stories about Nepenthe in the *Big Sur Roundup*.

A very warm thank-you to producer Martin Ransohoff. Our interview was one of the highlights of my research, and our phone conversations that followed always made me laugh. Thank you also to Joan Ransohoff. And to actress Eva Marie Saint, for kindly obliging to a phone interview.

To Brooke Elgie for lending photographs; to Joshua and Eliza Baer of the Morley Baer Photography Trust in Santa Fe, New Mexico, for the use of images; to Glen Cheda for the use of the Edmund Kara image; and to Monterey librarian Dennis Copeland for help with my research.

A special thank-you to Robin Burnside, for sharing stories and recipes, and your sweet friendship. To my stepmother, Elena Salsedo Steele, who taught me so much about good food and the pleasures of the table. Thanks to Alice Russell for sharing your part of our family story.

To Timothy Maiden for all your help regarding Nepenthe's architecture and for shedding light on our family's unique connections. To Bay area architects Henrik Bull and Pierluigi Serraino for your insights on Nepenthe's architecture and on the architect himself. To artist Marion Seawell for photos and remembrances of building the fireplace with my grandmother.

For on-the-ground daily support in Oakland, many, many thanks to Doug McKechnie for scanning images and always lending a hand; to Sukey Lilienthal and David Roe and family for so many acts of kindness and giving; to Susann Grody for caring. To David Houston and Mary Beaton for backup help at the drop of the hat; and to their daughter Gloria for being a part of our family. To the Bigotti family, for the love and care you have given Nicoya.

Thank you Judi Swinks for testing specific recipes and for our morning walks, and to Tricia O'Brien, my other walking partner and fellow writer.

For everything and all in between, for being themselves, to Trevor and Nicoya. This book is for you.

Many people barely received a passing mention in this book, or perhaps didn't make it into the story at all, but were thought of throughout the writing of it: the larger cast and crew (and children) of Nepenthe past and present, my grandparents' extensive collection of friends, and all my cousins and their children. Thank you all for being a part of the Nepenthe legacy.

In remembrance of Michele Peterson, longtime Phoenix Shop employee, who embodied my grandmother's spirit in so many ways and whose memory I drew on during the writing of this book, time and time again.

STAGE NOTES

Recipe Listing

Index

E

Eastwood, Clint   82, 230
eggs   note on xiii, 204–5, 238–39, 246–47
Elgie, Brooke   iv
Elliot, Mama Cass   117
Elliot, Ramblin' Jack   82
Emily   48, 227, 249
espresso machine   224
Europe. *See also* Capri, Italy
  food and   132
  tourism from   267
  travel to   132
Evans, Herb   181–82
Eyerman, J. R.   iv

F

family dinners   148, 298
family kitchen   131
  closing of   320
  description of   137
  gathering in   156, 218
  lunch in   148
  move of   227
  Sunday dinners in   154, 218
family traditions. *See also* holidays; family dinners
  Christmas   166–67, 170–71
  Thanksgiving   160
Farr, Fred   214
fashion shows   104, 105
Fassett, Dorcas Jane   3, 19, 80, 139, 322
  memories from   23, 160
  performances by   46, 47, 80
  work for   46
Fassett, Griff   3, 19, 139
  future for   57, 101
  memories from   37, 46, 154, 188
  work for   45
Fassett, Havrah   104, 230, 248, 249
Fassett, Holly   3, 19, 102, 191, 249, 293, 316, 322
  apple pie from   295
  at Bill's memorial   249
  cookies from   26
  on cream cheese pie   116
  desserts from   160, 298
  Halloween and   98
  hotcakes from   144
  as manager   182, 218, 223, 224, 249, 271
  memories from   37, 50, 55, 77, 88, 181, 214
  pie dough from   292
  work for   46
Fassett, Kaffe   3, 19, 101, 268, 322
  Christmas decorations from   166, 170

  for fashion   105, 107, 249
  knitting for   104
  memories from   37, 71
  performances by   80, 88
  for *The Sandpiper*   121–22
  work for   45
Fassett, Katie McCallie (Bill's sister)   19, 20
Fassett, Kim   3, 44, 201, 322
  Café Kevah and   235
  cake from   207
  performances by   88
  work for   46, 227
Fassett, Madeleine Adams Ulman (Lolly)   11, 83, 149, 157, 208, 322
  as Barefoot Contessa   13
  Bill v.   101, 104, 182, 230, 249
  for building   37
  on Capri   13
  care from   101, 132
  childhood of   9
  clothes for   154
  collecting for   23, 37, 103
  cooking style of   154, 155, 156, 162
  costumes from   98
  death of   213–15, 218
  dedication of   218
  on destiny   198
  Evans v.   181–82
  on future   218
  generosity of   60, 91, 101, 131–32, 154, 156, 160, 188, 213–14
  hotcakes from   144, 148
  lamb curry from   147
  management style of   77, 101, 127, 181–82
  memories from   4, 10, 13, 59, 218
  Monk on   77
  personality of   60, 77
  portrait of   212
  to residents   188
  restaurant's beginnings by   3–4
  The Sandpiper and   122
  skills from   132
  to staff   182
  staff on memorial of   213–14
  Sunday dinners from   154
  Trotter, Frank, for   213
  upstairs kitchen of   131
  wedding of   18, 19
Fassett, Newton Crocker   19
Fassett, Rosalyn   139
Fassett, William Elliot Griffis McCallie (Bill)   20, 83, 84, 231, 322
  childhood of   19